DOGANÇAY

Edited by

ROY MOYER

With an Introduction by

THOMAS M. MESSER

HHI

Hudson Hills Press

New York

FIRST EDITION

Preface ©1986 by Jacques Rigaud
Introduction ©1986 by Thomas M. Messer
Burhan Dogançay: His Life and Obsession ©1986 by Stephen DiLauro
Paintings and Graphics and Shadow Sculpture ©1986 by Roy Moyer
Photography—Walls of the World ©1986 by Gilbert Lascault
Afterword ©1986 by Clive Giboire

Published in the United States by Hudson Hills Press, Inc., Suite 1308, 230 Fifth Avenue, New York, NY 10001-7704.
Distributed in the United States by Rizzoli International Publications, Inc.
Distributed in Canada by Irwin Publishing Inc.
Distributed in the United Kingdom, Eire, Europe, Israel, and the Middle East by Phaidon Press Limited.
Distributed in Japan by Yohan (Western Publications Distribution Agency).

Produced for Hudson Hills Press by
TENTH AVENUE EDITIONS, INC.
885 Tenth Avenue, New York, NY 10019

Managing Editor: Clive Giboire
Associate Editors: Suzanne Gagné & Patricia Ann Higgins
Creative Director & Production Manager: Peter McKenzie

Typeset in Bembo by UGS Services/Universal Graphics Company, New York City
Printing, binding, and color separations by Industrie Grafiche Editoriali Fratelli Pagano S.p.A., Genoa, Italy

Library of Congress Cataloguing in Publication Data
Dogançay.

    Bibliography: p.
    1. Dogançay, Burhan, 1929–   —Addresses, essays,
lectures. I. Moyer, Roy, 1921–
N6537.D57D64 1986   709'.2'4   86-359
ISBN 0-933920-61-X

Front jacket illustration: SHADOW CASTING RIBBONS, 1985
                            Acrylic on canvas
                            48×71 ins. (122×180.3 cm.)

Back jacket illustration: POST NO BILLS, 1966
                           Gouache and collage on cardboard
                           29×21 ins. (73.7×53.3 cm.)

CONTENTS

ACKNOWLEDGMENTS

Burhan Dogançay and Tenth Avenue Editions, Inc. would like to thank Peter and Helga Endres for making this project possible; Dr. A. Odok, Dr. H. Severus and all the staff at the R & D Center of Swiss Aluminium Ltd. for their invaluable support; Dr. Pietro Alario of Industrie Grafiche Editoriali Fratelli Pagano S.p.A. for the great care he took at every stage of this book's production; and Christopher Turner and William Triplett for their useful suggestions and editorial assistance. Additional thanks go to the following photographers: Roland Brändli, D. James Dee, Ali Diblan, Önder Ergün, Hakkı Göceoglu, Carmelo Guadagno, Christoph Hauser, David Heald, W.G. Murray, E. Özbank, Nuri Özbudak, Sedat Pakay, and D. Savini. Credit is due to the Centre Georges Pompidou, Paris; The Chase Manhattan Bank, N.A., New York; the Georgia Museum of Art, The University of Georgia, Athens; The Newark Museum, Newark; The Snite Museum of Art, The University of Notre Dame, Notre Dame; The Solomon R. Guggenheim Museum, New York; and the State University College, Fredonia.

PREFACE

Burhan Dogançay's artistic development and work reflect a phenomenon characteristic of our times and invite meaningful comparisons with other major periods of artistic creation.

Hugo van der Goes, El Greco, and Claude Lorrain are three artists among many who traveled to Italy (from Flanders, Greece and France, respectively) and found there a school, an inspiration and a framework for highly personal syntheses. In a certain way this was also the case with Goethe, Corot and Berlioz. France played the same role for Leonardo and Rossini, as England did for Handel. European civilization would not be what it is without this complex game of exchange.

We all know what Europe was for Henry James, Mary Cassatt and Hemingway, or America for Stravinsky. Today, the adventure of creation takes place on a worldwide scale: witness the architect I. M. Pei. One of the great painters of our time, Zao Wou Ki, accomplished the synthesis of the great tradition of Chinese painting and contemporary abstract art in France.

It is against this background that Burhan Dogançay must be seen. Turkey is his fatherland, Europe his family, America his home. Among today's artists there are few examples of such vast and profound cosmopolitanism.

Dogançay does not deny his origins, and yet, it is not easy being a Turk. Wild and misunderstood, Turkey is the heir of a long, glorious and tragic history. For thousands of years Asia and Europe have confronted and been shaped by each other on this subcontinent, whose harsh plateaus evoke the infinite space of Asia as much as the soft riverbanks reflect Mediterranean harmony. Divided between fascination and repulsion, East and West coexist in this part of the world. It is Dogançay who achieved the impossible synthesis. He is as much at ease in Cairo and Istanbul as he is in Naples, Hamburg or Paris. Mediterranean clarity is his key to Eastern symbolism and Western rationality. A personal vision of tenderness and humor, with which he viewed in recent years the walls of big Eastern and Western cities, enabled him to give us these striking photographs that say more about our fantasies, our contradictions than could be said in lengthy speeches. Yet, these photographs are not only of documentary value; they also explain and introduce a highly original artistic oeuvre.

It is at this point that one must speak of America, because Dogançay's art owes almost everything to this country which received him and offered him a chance at true creative freedom. While the East represents an eternal balance between sensuous softness and aggressive harshness, America demands unity and coherence. Although sensuality and dreams are a part of America, efficiency and progress are what matter most.

In the early works of his American period one feels that Dogançay was firmly challenged by New York, that "upright" city, as Céline calls it, that city of metal, electricity and verticality like no other place in the world. The shock, the torn-apartness, the crowding, the fire: these are the rude assaults to which Dogançay's sensual and soft nature had to respond. The result is seen in his paintings and gouaches whose diversity does not obscure a profound unity. All his works are responses of courage and dignity to America's ceaseless and fertile aggression. Dogançay expresses in his own way the great adventure of all those who came to America in search of freedom. It is a tough apprenticeship to a generous but uncompromising society. Inevitably Charlie Chaplin comes to mind: the lonely, vulnerable man, pushed and jostled by the big city, and who, in the process of receiving one blow after another, fights back in his own way and finally finds the path to light and freedom.

JACQUES RIGAUD

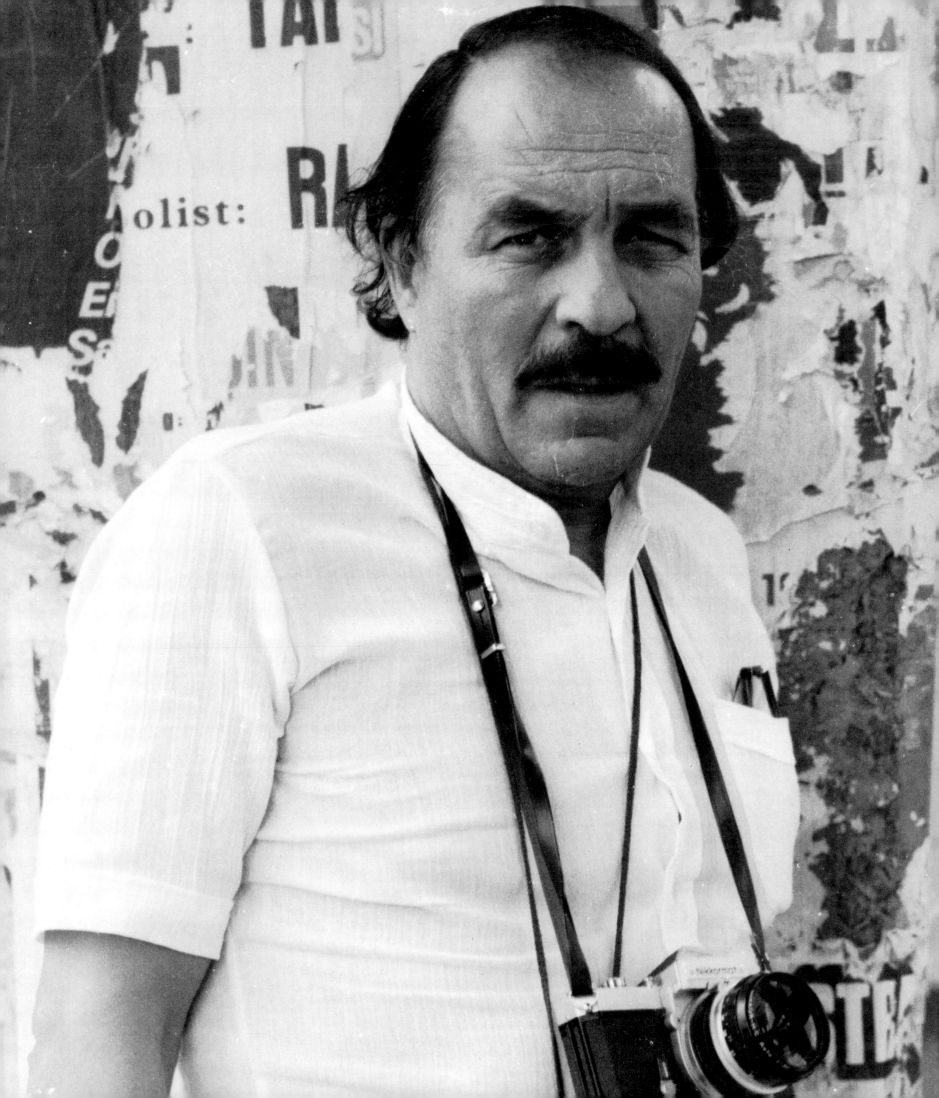

INTRODUCTION

When, in 1982, Burhan Dogançay showed his photographs of walls at the Centre Georges Pompidou in Paris, I wrote the following paragraphs for the exhibition catalogue:

> *Burhan Dogançay saw the walls, read and observed their surfaces, recorded, photographed, painted, compared, sorted and transformed their contents and used them as raw materials for his art. In doing so his sight sharpened as he became sensitive to the similarities and contrasts inherent in this medium of the untutored, a medium that consists of expressions in interplay with one another, as well as with the quickly changing appearance of its support. Dogançay's eye, attuned by the habit of observation, became capable of distinguishing between meaningful and meaningless constellations, between evocative and neutral imagery, between walls capable of returning to the attentive viewer something of their substance and others without such capacity.*
>
> *The photographs assembled here will enrich us in two separate ways: first, by providing a quintessential selection of the artist's involvement—as a digest, in other words, that will allow us to see the most that may be extracted through the artist's eyes. Beyond this, Dogançay's photographs will serve as an introduction to his art. For the paintings, gouaches and prints Dogançay has produced in years of diligent and creative work, while no longer necessarily referring to the wall language, have drawn strength from his mural insights, so assiduously cultivated. Burhan Dogançay's contribution thus may be seen as an extension of a collective vernacular, transformed into art, as defined by a unique individual sensibility.*

And so, his paintings and work on paper, like the walls he was preoccupied with for years, are also essentially a dialogue with flatness. Paper and canvas grounds, having been substituted for the mural medium, are now inviting brush and pen to perform as if these tools and the imagery they conjure up were consummate dancers capable of a wide range of expressive movement. There are black strokes on black that barely lift themselves from the ground that harbors them before they erupt in starkly contrasting red and yellow stripes as if executing a complex jeté. In other instances, tinted grays establish an accommodating link between the whiteness of the paper and brushstrokes of glaringly contrasting hues.

The painted shapes retain the *illusion* of torn paper as they emerge *trompe l'oeil* fashion from a *real* paper ground. Reality and illusion, in that time-honored interplay, find a new application in Dogançay's complex convolutions as they proceed from their nervous pointed inception toward a harmonious conclusion.

Burhan Dogançay has not appeared from nowhere, nor is that mastery he has attained of recent vintage. It was my privilege to observe his growth and development as an artist over a period of twenty years during which his forms have simplified, his volumes have grown more ample and his expressive strength has intensified. Much as with many calligraphers from Eastern lands, Dogançay's subject remains the same, but its rendition depends each time upon his capacity for self-renewal. His coloristic pirouettes, suggestive of the futility and the ephemeral nature of human gestures, carry his art beyond an ornamental exercise.

THOMAS M. MESSER

BURHAN DOGANÇAY:

His Life and Obsession

The artist today becomes unreal if he remains in his ivory tower or sterilized if he spends his time galloping around the political arena. Yet between the two lies the arduous way of true art.

—ALBERT CAMUS

For the past twenty years Burhan Doğançay has extensively and obsessively explored the subject of walls in his paintings, graphics, photographs, and most recently in his sculptures. While other contemporary artists have used walls as their subject matter, few have been as consistent as Doğançay in pursuing the theme. In every medium he has brought an elegance to his chosen subject. Doğançay has claimed walls—with their solid presence, their universal graffiti—and created for them a kind of permanence that they otherwise would never have.

Doğançay was born September 11, 1929, in Istanbul and was raised in Ankara, Turkey. From childhood Doğançay showed a talent for living that would foster and enrich his dream of becoming an artist. He was good at everything he did: he excelled at school, effortlessly taking a degree in law at the University of Ankara (he would have preferred to study architecture, but the curriculum was not available); he played professional soccer with the Genclerbirligi, leading the team to two national championships; he attained the rank of *sous lieutenant* in the military, serving with his father, a major; he was the first member of his family to study in the West, receiving a doctorate in economics in Paris; by 1962, he was Director of Information and Tourism in the U.S., enjoying full diplomatic status. That he eventually chose art as his profession is in a way remarkable. Yet in 1964, he turned himself over to it entirely, relinquishing all titles, status, and societal immunities and guarantees.

His change from career diplomat to artist, which shocked his family and his country's elite, was not as abrupt as it might seem, for Doğançay had painted throughout his life. His father, Adil Doğançay, a career military man, was a cartographer, who, like other artists, used pen and colored inks in his work. He took his son on map-making expeditions throughout Turkey, and the two traveled caravan-style with foot soldiers, camping on the steppes or on some high plateau. When not on duty, the father often sketched and painted. When his young son took an interest in art, Adil and his friends helped the boy along, showing him how to handle light, shadow, and perspective.

During his high-school days, Doğançay studied after class with the well-known Turkish painter, Arif Kaptan, who gave him training in classical art, with a special emphasis on drawing Greek statuary from various angles. Both Kaptan and Adil Doğançay strongly believed that drawing was the basis of good painting.

Doğançay as a child

Despite his preference for architecture—and despite his lack of attention to his professors, of whom he drew caricatures during lectures—Dogançay, rather to his surprise, received a degree in law. At this point his compulsory military service loomed before him. While deciding whether to go straight into the service or to practice law, he took up gambling, spending a great deal of time with jockeys, trainers, handlers, and owners, whose idiosyncracies might make or break a race. He then entered the military somewhat grudgingly, remaining a rebel at first. However, in a country where soccer is a national passion, his abilities were widely recognized, and his behavior, for the most part, was overlooked.

As a young man Adil Dogançay had dreamed of studying in Europe, but World War I and Turkey's war for independence quashed any hope of that. The elder Dogançay wished to fulfill his dreams through his son, but first secured two promises from him: one, Burhan had to promise that he would not play professional soccer, and two, that he would not allow his interest in art to distract him from his doctoral studies—Adil Dogançay was sure there was no place in this world for a Turk who thought he was an artist. At worst, his son would be in the company of Kandinsky, Matisse, and Courbet, all of whom had law degrees.

Realizing that the financing of his European studies was going to be a burden on his family, Dogançay made these promises to his father. In January 1950 the

Dogançay sketching in
Montmartre, Paris, 1953

Dogançay family gathered at the pier in Istanbul to see the first of their family leave for the West.

Arriving in Paris, Dogançay enrolled at the Alliance Française and La Grande Chaumière and lived at the American House at the Cité Universitaire. He continued to sketch and paint, and one of his many subjects was the house of Dr. Gachet, patron and friend of the Impressionists, at Auvers-sur-Oise. He was also moved by a visit to the nearby graves of Theo and Vincent van Gogh.

Dogançay was soon surrounded by friends from the East, and he also made American friends in the dormitory; however, he was not mingling enough with French people to learn the language. By a stroke of luck, he got a paying part as a stand-in for Ronald Shiner, the famous British comedian, in the movie *Weekend in Paris*. With this money, and funds saved from other part-time jobs such as night-clerking at the American House, he was able to support himself without the aid of his family for a while. He took the opportunity to spend a year painting and learning French in the village of Honfleur—a mecca for artists since the days of the Impressionist school—in the province of Normandy. His skill at soccer was his entrée into local society, and the vigor and beauty of his early paintings were praised by his new friends—local high school teachers from whom he learned French.

HONFLEUR, 1951
Watercolor on paper,
10 × 13 ins. (25.4 × 33 cm.)

Paris, 1952

He returned to Paris, leaving his life as a painter reluctantly and, he knew, temporarily. In his heart he realized that he would some day devote himself exclusively to art, but he also had dues to pay and he paid them, finally sending a telegram to his parents: "Greetings. Finished. Your son, Dr. Dogançay."

While finishing his doctoral thesis, "Coopération et les Progrès de l'Agriculture Danoise," Dogançay took part in a group show called *Exposition des Peintres Résidants de la Fondation des Etats-Unis*. His economics professors attended and insisted that his artistic talent demanded that he become an artist. Dogançay replied: "The economics of art is hunger," a truth which he would some day experience.

On his return to Ankara, Dogançay became chief of staff for the Undersecretary of Commerce. The pay was low, but the undersecretary at that time was Munis F. Ozansoy, a leading Turkish poet and man of letters as well as an art lover, who took an immediate interest in Dogançay's work and arranged a joint show for father and son at the Sanatsevenler Club in Ankara. The cultural and social elite of Ankara were invited, along with members of the government and the foreign diplomatic corps.

Many paintings were sold, and there was considerable critical acclaim: the *Zafer*, a leading daily paper in Ankara, said, "The talk of art circles here is that if Burhan Dogançay should ever devote himself exclusively to painting, Turkey will have its first internationally renowned artist." In the guest book, the painter Ihsan C. Karaburçak wrote: "I am one hundred percent sure that one day Burhan's desire to paint will overwhelm him and he will give up every other occupation to fulfill his true calling." These encouraging comments, and the equally encouraging proceeds from the brisk sale of the paintings, cheered him on.

Throughout the late fifties Dogançay continued to work for the government: in 1956 he was appointed commissioner of the Izmir International Trade Fair; in 1958 he was appointed director of the Turkish pavilion at the Brussels Exposition Universelle et Internationale; by 1959 he was appointed Director General of Tourism, a job which took him all over the world. The first member of the Dogançay family to study in the West had now become a citizen of the world.

Ever a sportsman, he also served for two years as general manager of his old soccer club. When in 1962 he was allowed to choose his own post abroad, his friends and family expected him to return to Paris, but instead he chose New York City, going at last to America, of which he had long dreamed.

Life in America was filled with long days of work on the fifty-eighth floor of 500 Fifth Avenue and long nights of parties, yachting, and embassy dinners. But even so Dogançay found time to sketch and paint, keeping a sketchbook in his office and even returning at night to paint the Manhattan skyline. In 1963

NUDE, 1951
Crayon on paper, 6 × 6 ins. (15.2 × 15.2 cm.)

MY LANDLADY'S CAT, 1951
Crayon and India ink on paper, 9 × 6 ins. (22.9 × 15.2 cm.)

VAGRANT, 1951
Charcoal on paper,
7 × 10¾ ins. (17.8 × 27.3 cm.)

at the *World Show* at the Washington Square Galleries, Dogançay's paintings were reviewed by L.E. Levick, a critic from the *New York Journal American*. Dogançay was pleased and surprised to see his name mentioned with Andy Warhol, Willem de Kooning, Larry Rivers, and Louise Nevelson. Dogançay also took part in a group show at the National Arts Club on Gramercy Park the same year.

It was at this time that his fascination with walls began. Having broken through all the boundaries of his personal life and culture, Dogançay could treasure walls for the ephemera they were—and still are. The transient surfaces, loaded with the marks of time and passing strangers, developed an urgency new to Dogançay.

Then the government informed him that he was being posted to Paris. He refused the assignment, took three months' accumulated leave, and then resigned. He began to paint with a passion and a sense of freedom previously unknown to him. Dogançay had gambled before, and he gambled again, wandering endlessly, searching the city for walls that would speak. In 1964, Ward Eggleston Galleries presented his first one-man show. Also in 1964, New York City celebrated its tricentennial, and as part of the celebration, Dogançay had a one-man show at the Berlitz School Galleries entitled *New York in the Eyes of the World*. He displayed eighty-two works, including the new wall paintings as well as the cityscapes for which he had previously been known. Again the work was well received, and Mayor Wagner awarded him a Certificate of Appreciation.

When Dogançay rejected his government career, the telephone stopped ringing and all invitations ceased. Still his work was being shown and sold, so all seemed well. In March 1965 he had another show at the Ward Eggleston Galleries; this time, though the critics praised the work, it did not sell. Shortly after Ward Eggleston closed its doors, the real struggle to stay alive in the city began. In 1966 an exhibition at the American Greetings Gallery in the Pan Am Building, in which new wall paintings appeared, received a lot of publicity—even television coverage—but not one of the artworks sold.

Desperation and loneliness began. There was no money coming in and Dogançay faced repeated, humiliating rejections of his work. Gallery owners hardly bothered to look at the slides of his artwork, let alone the work itself. Moreover his government was constantly trying to entice him back into service and his parents pressured him to accept. Offsetting the strain and struggle, a number of his paintings were acquired by museums and corporate collections.

Just when Dogançay actually considered returning to Turkey, Thomas M. Messer, director of The Solomon R. Guggenheim Museum, urged him to remain. "You've only devoted yourself completely to art for the past five years. Do you have any idea how long it took for the great masters to gain recognition?" he asked. Dogançay wanted to know how one was to make a living, but Messer simply remarked that all the great artists answered that question by continuing to work. "In my opinion you would be a fool to give up now," he added. Dogançay persevered.

Dogançay painting a portrait, Paris, 1952

Father and son at joint exhibition, Ankara, 1957

Father and son at joint exhibition, Istanbul, 1983

CALCUTTA, 1959
Watercolor and India ink on paper, 9 × 12 ins. (22.9 × 30.5 cm.)

Adil Dogançay, STILL LIFE, 1959
Oil on Masonite, 17¾ × 14¾ ins. (45.1 × 37.5 cm.)

HASAN, 1952
Watercolor on paper, 15 × 11 ins. (38.1 × 27.9 cm.)

Meanwhile Roy Moyer, at that time director of the American Federation of Arts, who had borrowed several of Dogançay's new gouaches depicting walls, called to tell him he had shown the works to Henry Geldzahler, then head of the twentieth-century art department at the Metropolitan Museum of Art. Geldzahler secured a fellowship for Dogançay at the Tamarind Lithography Workshop in Los Angeles. This important fellowship marked a turning point in Dogançay's career: he was a seasoned artist who had faced the nearly impossible challenge of living by his art, and succeeded.

Between 1960 and 1970 approximately seventy artists attended the Tamarind Workshop, a ten-year project conceived to promote lithography in America. Dogançay participated in 1969. There, he created seventeen lithographs, including a suite of eleven impressions titled *Walls V*. Gallery shows followed in New York City and throughout the U.S. In 1970 he executed a portfolio of sixteen lithographs called *Walls 70* at the Bank Street Atelier in Manhattan, a project in which Randy Rosen was instrumental. At about the same time the late Daniel C. Rich, a trustee of The Solomon R. Guggenheim Museum, began to take an interest in Dogançay's gouache/fumage technique, which employed candle smoke to shade painted surfaces. This direct, elemental approach resulted in an immediate, real, yet subtle effect.

In 1977 he began to show his paintings in Europe and created a suite of four lithographs, *Walls 77*, at the Wolfsberg Lithography Workshop in Zurich, Switzerland. There also were shows in Istanbul, where he exhibited (and still exhibits to this day) with his father, in Sweden and West Germany, and at the Gimpel and Weitzenhoffer Gallery in New York. Today Dogançay's paintings hang in museums and private collections in many different parts of the world.

Dogançay met Angela Hausmann, a graduate of the University of Geneva and the City University of New York, in 1972, and their marriage in 1978 marked the beginning of a durable and sustaining relationship.

Dogançay's obsession with walls grew more intense. Beginning in 1972 his desire to capture the moments in time when walls achieve a perfection of anonymous communication led him on a worldwide photographic quest. From 1972 till 1982 he amassed an archive of over twelve thousand transparencies preserving moments of love, hate, desperation, and ennui in North and South America, parts of Asia and Africa, and all across Western Europe. In 1982 a selection of these photographs was presented at the Centre Georges Pompidou in Paris. The show, *Les murs murmurent, ils crient, ils chantent...*, then traveled through France, Belgium, and Canada. The pictures firmly established Dogançay's reputation as a photographer.

HOUSE OF DR. GACHET, 1953
Gouache and India ink on paper
8 × 5 ins. (20.3 × 12.7 cm.)

For some time Dogançay had been making small maquettes to achieve accurate shapes and shadows in his paintings. When Thomas Messer saw some of these in 1980, he suggested that Dogançay try his hand at sculpture. By 1983 Dogançay's first public sculpture appeared, fashioned from Alucobond, a new material developed by Swiss Aluminium Ltd., in Zurich, that consists of thin sheets of aluminum alloy bonded to hard black polyethylene. The Swiss company, which normally supplies products for heavy industry and construction, was, nevertheless, delighted to collaborate with an artist in making a series of shadow sculptures. The result was yet another important step in Dogançay's evolution in communicating his obsession.

In 1983 Maître Picaud of L'Atelier Raymond Picaud in Aubusson came to see Dogançay's gouaches and decided to reproduce some of the work in tapestry form. To date six original Dogançay tapestries have been created.

Since 1983 Dogançay has moved away from pure documentation and observation. The artist as speaker has emerged: the painted walls are no longer realistic flat collages. They have started to explode. Unlike Warhol's surfaces, which are all surface, Dogançay's surfaces are all depth.

Dogançay lives and works in New York City and makes several trips abroad each year, documenting walls wherever he goes. The walls' messages of love, sex, and politics, each one unique and personal to the writer yet everywhere the same, attest to a common bond between all people. It is this universality of human sentiment that Dogançay has appreciated, preserved, and transformed, creating artworks from the spontaneous expression of passing strangers.

STEPHEN DiLAURO

Adil Dogançay, WINTER IN ANKARA, 1958
Oil on Masonite, 19½ × 16 ins. (49.5 × 40.6 cm.)

AFTER THE STORM, 1959
Watercolor on paper, 6 × 10 ins. (15.2 × 25.4 cm.)

LEXINGTON AND 55TH AT NIGHT, 1963
Watercolor on paper, 20 × 15 ins. (50.8 × 38.1 cm.)

53RD STREET AT THIRD AVENUE, 1963
Watercolor on paper, 18 × 12 ins. (45.7 × 30.5 cm.)

MANHATTAN AND NEW JERSEY AT NIGHT, 1962
Watercolor on paper, 18 × 14 ins. (45.7 × 35.6 cm.)

New York
Journal American
Pictorial Living
JANUARY 3, 1965

A FOREIGN DIPLOMAT
PAINTS NEW YORK
(SEE PAGE 6)

A CORNER IN BROOKLYN by Burhan Dogançay

CORNER IN BROOKLYN, cover: *The New York Journal American*, 1964
Gouache on paper, 22 × 20 ins. (55.9 × 50.8 cm.)
Private collection, New York

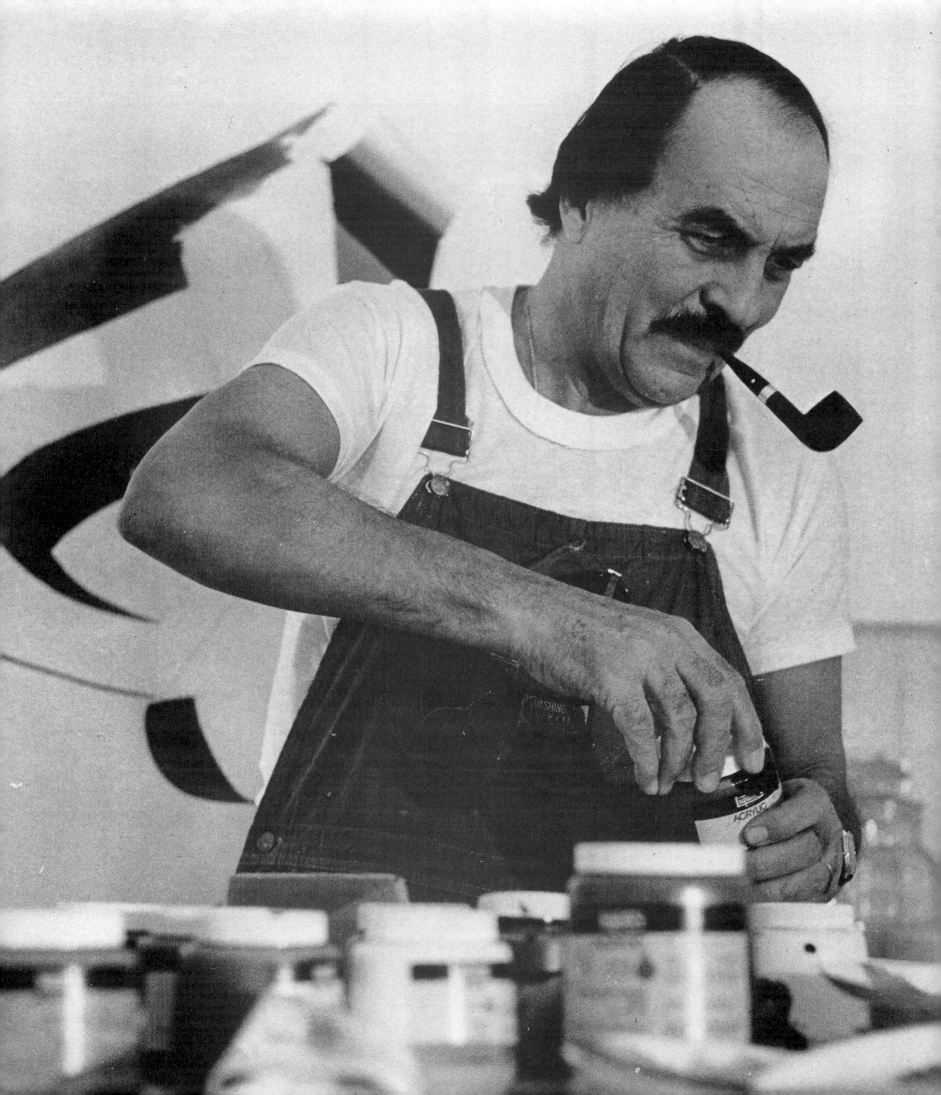

INTERVIEW

The following is an excerpt from an interview between Marcel van Jole, esteemed member of the International Association of Art Critics, and Burhan Dogançay, which took place in Brussels during February 1983.

MvJ: *When you are standing in front of an empty canvas, do you know what the painting that fills it will be like?*

BD: Yes, most of the time. First, I build a paper model. Using it as a basis, I create a fundamental design in which the important elements—lines, "tear-ups," shadows—form a harmonious composition. As you know, lines and composition are the foundations of my work and I have little margin in which to correct errors. Mostly, I want to create a three-dimensional effect.

MvJ: *Can you interrupt painting a canvas and then resume working on it several months later?*

BD: Yes. But, in general, I try to finish a canvas as soon as possible.

MvJ: *Is it sometimes difficult to part with a painting that you like very much?*

BD: On the one hand, I try to keep my favorites, which is not always possible. On the other hand, it always makes me feel good to see a painting which was hard to part with hanging in a public or private collection.

MvJ: *Do you ever try to paint that so-called "unique" canvas, which makes all the others superfluous, a kind of synthetic painting which Picasso tried to accomplish for eighty years?*

BD: Quite frankly, that approach to art is very different from my own.

MvJ: *Have your trips to Europe and your living in the United States affected your approach to art?*

BD: Yes, definitely. Had van Gogh, for example, remained all his life in Holland or Belgium without going to France, his color palette might not have been the same. Art must have, and it always has had, a connection with the environment in which it is created. In my case, I doubt I ever would have become so obsessed with walls if I hadn't come to New York City.

MvJ: *When you arrive in a city for the first time, how do you find graffiti? Who or what indicates where you might find them?*

BD: Walking endless hours is the key. But, after twenty years, I have developed a sharp sense for it. Whenever I get desperate, though, I always head straight for the nearest university.

MvJ: *A large number of your early works were collages based on the wall theme. Why did you stop making these?*

BD: Like many contemporary artists, I was intrigued by collage. For me it was a natural medium because twentieth-century walls are themselves huge collages. The materials I used were often dirty posters and papers taken from actual walls. Collage was a logical step toward the effect of three dimensions in my recent and current work.

MvJ: *Do you feel the need to show your work? Would you be able to work in an egocentric way, only for your own pleasure?*

BD: This has been a rather controversial question among artists for many years. Since art is my only source of income, I have no other alternative but to expose my work to the public in an attempt to sell. Also, I believe—even though many artists are not willing to accept this—it is every artist's aim and ambition to be recognized by the public. But, I also do drawings, gouaches and watercolors sometimes purely for pleasure and I don't show these to anyone. They are hiding in the closet, so to speak.

MvJ: *Photography has influenced considerably the art of painting. As someone who has achieved recognition in both these fields, how do you feel about the influence of the new medium upon the old? Is it positive or negative?*

BD: Very positive. Many well-known painters used photographs as a basis for their paintings. Without photographic postcards, many of Utrillo's beautiful scenes of Montmartre might not have been possible. Degas was greatly interested in photography, as were Cézanne and Dali. Nowadays, Photo-Realism would not be possible without photography.

MvJ: *Do you believe it is possible to forecast which works and trends of today's art will be significant in ten, twenty, or thirty years, and which will be the currents and personalities that will force themselves on art historians in the future?*

BD: I am not a fortune-teller. But, looking at the history of art, I believe the paintings that are in the "courts" of today (i.e., corporations, rich museums, the homes of wealthy and powerful collectors) stand an excellent chance of being passed on to future generations.

But, I do not know whether these paintings will go down in art history as masterpieces. Increased competition among museums and big established collections in their endless search for something new and sensational has led to an accumulation of rather mediocre art.

MvJ: *Do you like to talk about art with your contemporaries?*

BD: Very seldom. I prefer to produce instead of talking or arguing endlessly about either my own or other artists' work.

MvJ: *Aside from painting, which natural gift would you most like to possess?*

BD: Don't you think it's enough to have the talent of a painter?

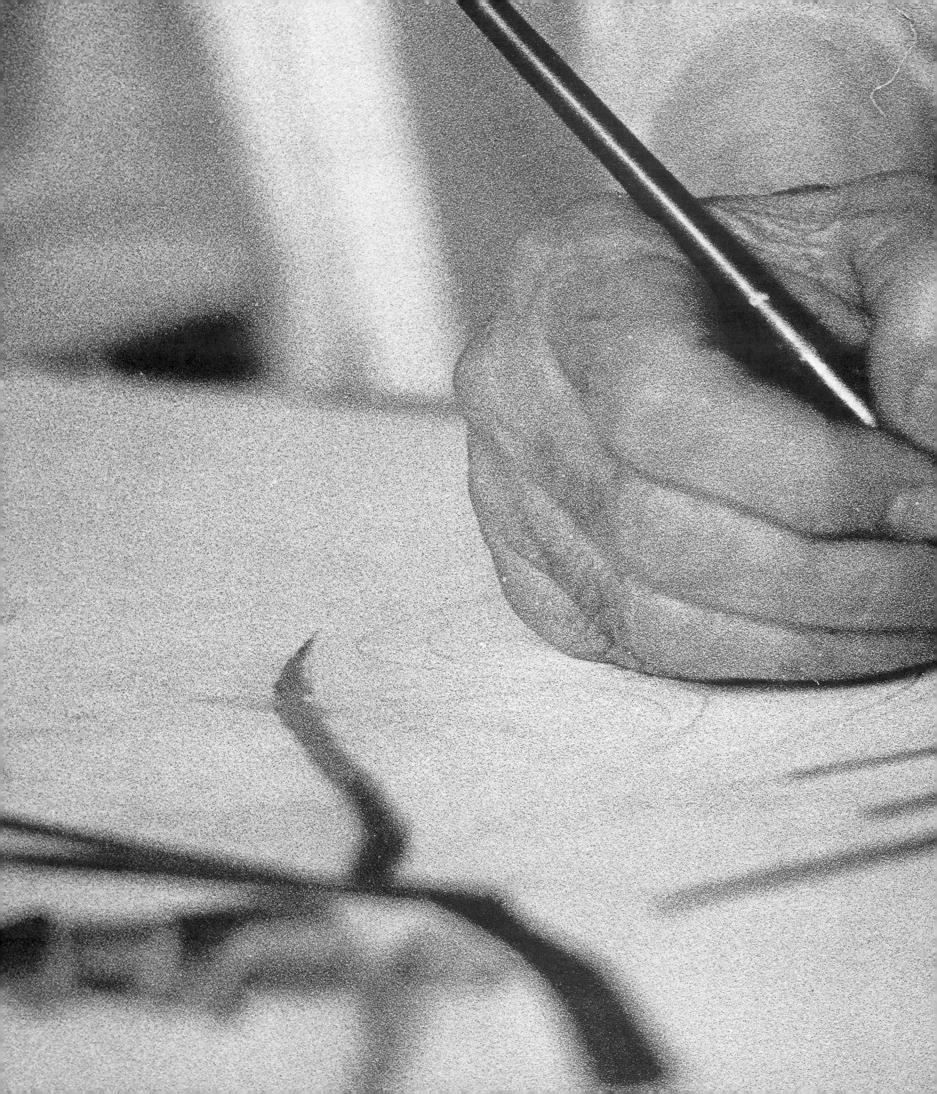

PAINTINGS
and
GRAPHICS

No matter what is the nationality of the artist, the spirit of the place is imprinted on his work. On the other hand no matter where the artist paints, his nationality is reflected in his work.
—JOHN GRAHAM

Burhan Dogançay's ability to create an individual image that is in keeping with both international aesthetics and with traditional calligraphic art forms of his native Turkey reveals a modern awareness coupled with personal integrity that have resulted in a powerful and beautiful synthesis.

In Eastern Mediterranean tradition, architecture and writing are uniquely intertwined: the mass of the wall is graced by script. A union unknown in Western art is thereby formed; it is a continuation of both ancient hieroglyph and cuneiform: the speaking wall. Dogançay's sensitivity to the present made him see this speaking wall first as a public forum and later as a private statement. In so doing, he transformed the anonymous into the personal, and what was once profane, transient, and humorous has become profound and subtle.

Dogançay's development as an artist has always been related to his interest in public walls as a form of mural art, which he admired for its spontaneity, directness, and temporal relevance. His early paintings, seemingly literal renditions on canvas of urban walls, were an attempt to record both evidences of history and, by indirection, personal feeling. This theme has continued throughout his career as he progressed from observer and recorder of these walls to become a painter who is confidently expressive of his own emotions. It has culminated in sculptures that are, in effect, walls he himself builds.

The relation between paintings and walls, or between studio easel paintings and mural paintings, is an intriguing one to artists, because it raises the question of the difference between private visual analysis and public statement. Yet the artist who paints for himself as a means of exploring his personal growth is also torn by his desire to declare his feelings publicly. This ambiguity of artistic intent—the sensitivity of artistic perception and the insensitivity of public declaration—coalesces and resolves itself in Dogançay's paintings whose subject matter is public walls.

Any subject is a suitable one for a public wall. When a scribbler writes his message of love on a wall, he is like the artist in his desire to share a very personal secret feeling with an anonymous audience, which incongruously confronts it only in passing. The public does not "go to" the wall as a deliberate experience, as one would go to an exhibition to see paintings; instead, the wall is an accidental intrusion into one's daily life, the medium for a brash public declaration of a private emotion.

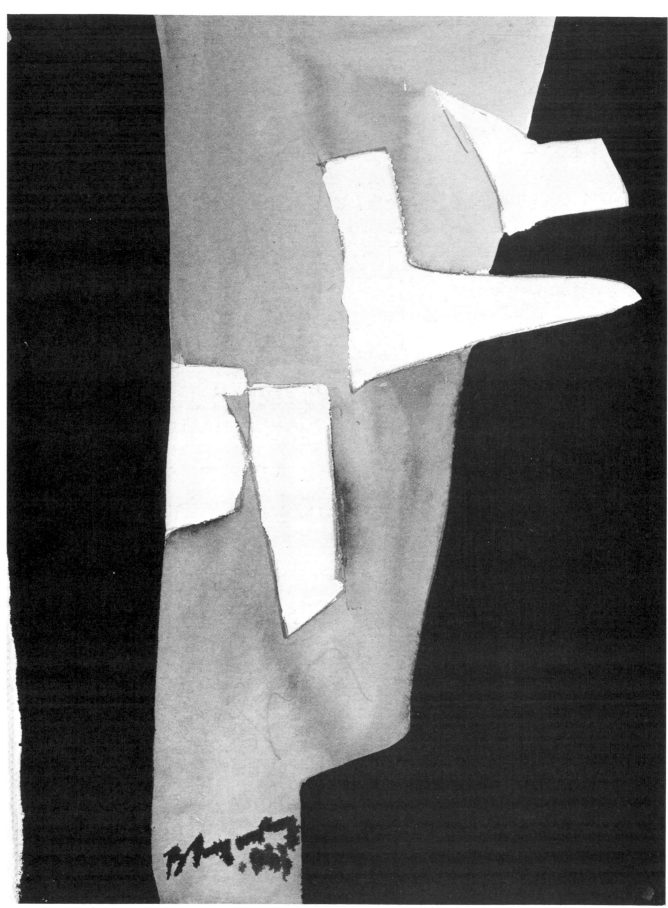

SHADOWS ON THE WALL, 1963
Gouache on paper, 15 × 11 ins. (38.1 × 27.9 cm.)

BILLBOARD, 1964
Gouache and collage on cardboard, 22⅛ × 19¾ ins. (56.2 × 50.2 cm.)
Collection The Solomon R. Guggenheim Museum, New York

47

Since anyone can write on a wall, can cross out other messages, peel off posters and change their meaning, many authors can be involved. Thus the factor of time also works on a wall in a way that time does not work on a painting, so that the message on the wall may contain the poignancy of the fading rose or the folly of contradictory injunctions or appeals. Walls have proved to be an ideal expression of the conflicts of life, the passing of feelings, even the effects of time and weather upon the concerns of the moment, and one is struck by the impermanence of passion and the ironies of layers of life contrasted by chance.

In his early works Doğançay succeeded in creating a pictorial continuum of image, background wall, and words. Their memorable character showed that irony was essential to his approach to subject matter. Employing what seemed, at first glance, to be objective reportage, the artist gave an impression of being aloof and unromantic, regarding his subject matter as dispassionately as still life. The intense irony that resulted from his apparently uninvolved portrayal of walls related his paintings of the 1960s to Pop Art, and his work seemed to show a neutrality of emotion similar to that expressed in the Dadaist *objet trouvé*. In reality, he carefully chose subject matter that juxtaposed naive and children's art with the most sophisticated forms of advertising and political statements, or he used found objects, puns, and words crossed out that either heightened or obscured meaning. When words are crossed out or changed, one is aware of both the original intent

YANKEES AND BEATLES, 1964
Gouache on cardboard, 18 × 27 ins. (45.7 × 68.6 cm.)

and the newer, modified significance, creating a sense of transience. So although his method was to present his subject matter as if he were an uninvolved observer, his choice of subject matter in fact implied emotional involvement. His work occasionally showed a mordant wit, but all of his work is an exploration of his concern with the tragic, the defaced, the false, and the abandoned. This includes his most recent paintings, where ribbons burst through the surface of a wall like pent-up emotions spilling toward the observer: delicate, gentle ribbons whose explosive life force makes them seem like plant tendrils that can burst through metal.

What lies beyond the wall? It is remarkable that Dogançay is able to make one dream of events that are not depicted by stimulating one's curiosity to look beyond surface appearances. Instead of being easily read, the wall can be a facade, a deceit, an exclusion, an impasse, an unyielding beginning of privacy. Using the surface of the painting to entice one to speculate about what is not shown, Dogançay employs a teasing ambiguity between the front and the back of the canvas. In his most recent works the back explodes through the front. These paintings have exchanged literal subject matter for more generalized universal feelings. Here the bursting tension of elegant forms and colors replaces the tension he previously created through juxtaposed messages.

In both his early and late works, however, Dogançay portrays the evidences of passions and events at a moment when the events are over. His works are re-

NO PAR KING, 1966
Oil on canvas, 24 × 30 ins. (61 × 76.2 cm.)

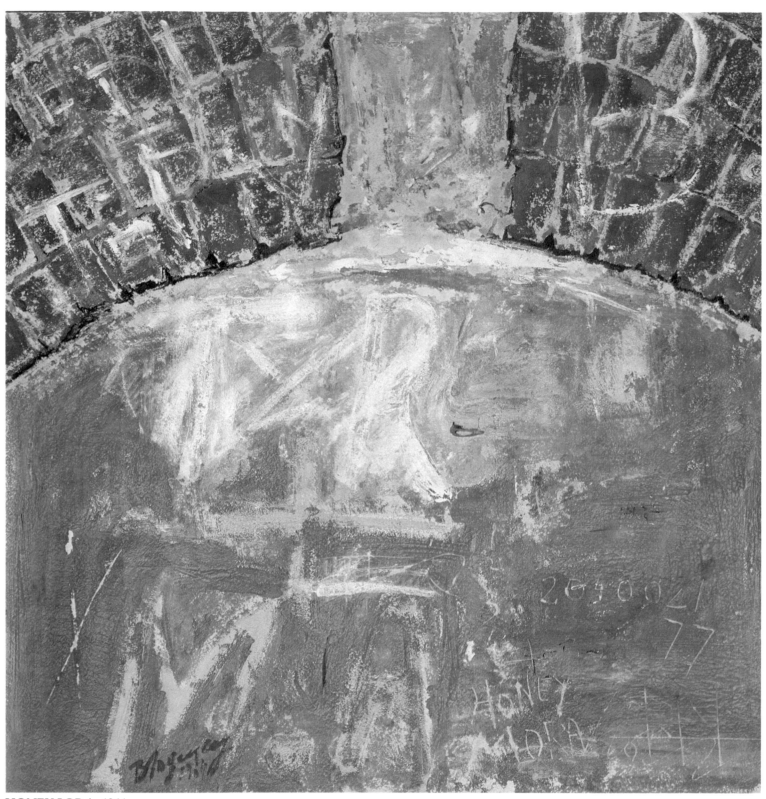

HONEY LORA, 1964
Gouache on cardboard, 24 × 24 ins. (61 × 61 cm.)
Private collection, Chappaqua, New York

CARLO LOVES, 1964
Gouache and collage on cardboard, 19½ × 25 ins. (49.5 × 63.5 cm.)

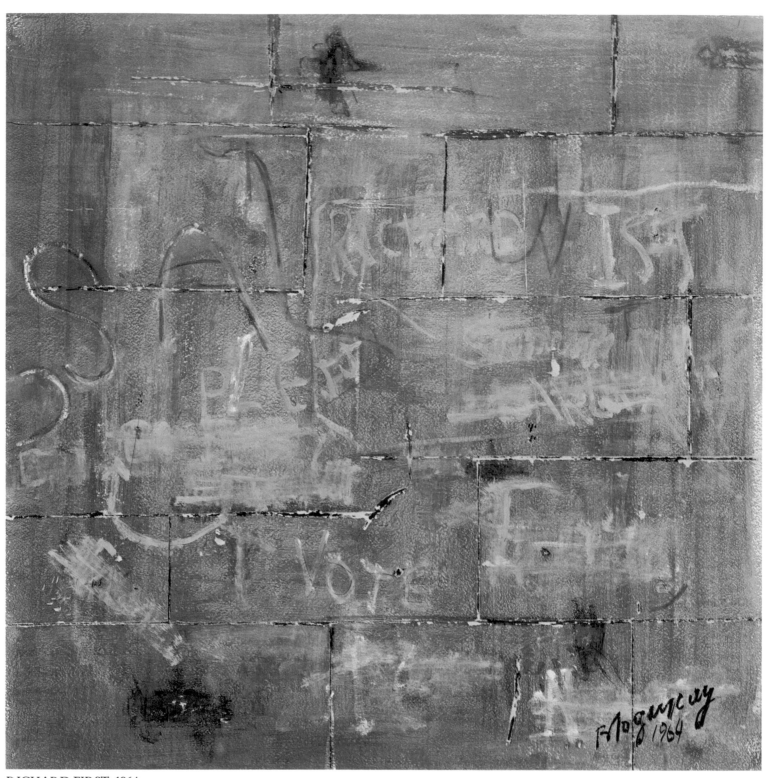

RICHARD FIRST, 1964
Gouache on cardboard, 26 × 26 ins. (66 × 66 cm.)

flections upon what had been, revealing the debris or wreckage left when feeling has ended. It is consistent with this reflective, investigative, detective-like approach to interpreting evidence that he would become concerned with smoke rather than fire.

In the early 1970s Doğançay created a series of paintings in which the surfaces appeared scorched and smoke-stained. These paintings reveal a method of dealing with emotions that are too great to be confronted at the time and must be considered in reflection after they have begun to subside. Other paintings show attempts to repair disaster: pieces are glued back together and recomposed, but incorrectly or ineptly and haphazardly, as if nothing that is once broken can ever be correctly repaired.

These are city paintings evoking the decay and destruction of the city, the alienated feeling that urban life is in ruins and out of control, and that we cannot put the pieces together again. They project the feeling that aborted emotions, false promises, and hopelessness cannot be mended in one's own life. The desire to deface, (which is implicit in graffiti) reflects both a societal and an individual sense of ruin.

In this artistic process, the artist employs the wall as a metaphor for a contemporary malaise. He does this to show that both internally and externally things are falling apart. Like the wall, one has been abraded, defaced, made impersonal; one senses a crowd of unseen people who find as little hope in correctly fitting their internal pieces back together as they do in putting the external pieces of the world in order.

How did Doğançay transform his early literal reportage into a personally expressive and distinctive art? His first paintings often depicted walls on which old political campaign posters were torn away to be replaced by advertisements for cabaret acts; political figures were turned into comedians with the addition of obscene comments and false moustaches; and signs advertising antiques blotted out the images of almost forgotten political figures. Children's scribbles and stick figures were juxtaposed with colorful and sophisticated abstract shapes remaining from layers of torn posters. The abstractions that resulted from ambiguous written messages and colorful fragments of now-unreadable images were a form of abstract expressionism based upon the laws of chance. Here was abstract expressionism acted upon by the elements, painted by nature herself and selected by the artist for its casual beauty. In these early works, he was able to play upon two important elements of modern art: the beauty of chance composition and an existential message.

Doğançay found a way to resolve message and abstraction, each having an equal

COMMUNICATION, 1965
Oil and mixed media on canvas,
50 × 50 ins. (127 × 127 cm.)

WEST SIDE STORY, 1964
Gouache and collage on cardboard, 19½ × 25 ins. (49.5 × 63.5 cm.)
Private collection, Geneva

MICHAEL AND MARY, 1964
Gouache on cardboard, 28 × 28 ins. (71.1 × 71.1 cm.)

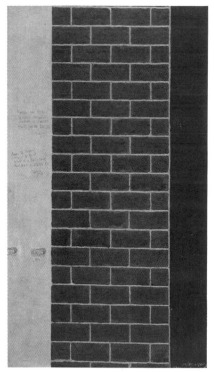

BROWNSTONE, 1966
Oil on canvas,
50 × 28 ins. (127 × 71.1 cm.)

circumstantial existence, and he became the interpreter and preserver of the fleeting moment. Many of the recorded messages are about hearts and love. The word *love* was tenderly written or engraved and embellished upon a door secured with a lock. It was scratched out, misspelled, or unplanned and cramped. Names of lovers were crossed out and replaced, and the word *love* was sometimes blotted out with pornography. To Dogançay these messages were terse reflections of his own perceptions of the innocent, the vulgar, and the transient aspects of relationships.

In this regard, one remembers the Biblical concept of writing on the wall as a warning—a prophecy of doom and disaster. This creates a special moral astringency in the artist's use of such words as *liberty* and *love*. Dogançay comes from a culture where writing on the wall of the mosque was traditionally a revelation of the existence of God. In the West today, writing is often the contract, the promise, the decree that is forgotten, changed, eroded. There is a contrast between the sacred and eternal quality of Islamic script and the relative and existential meaning of words today. Writing from the Koran, spread upon the walls, proclaims eternal truth; modern journalistic writing may instead proclaim the eternal lie. Dogançay's paintings reveal the corruption of words and the substitution of deception for truth.

In a poignant way, these paintings act as signposts, guides, and warnings: political leaders are crossed out with dripping red paint, and beneath the confession of love is an arrow advising a detour. In general, what begins as the bright, enticing advertising of products or feelings turns bitter, regretful, and disappointed. It is clear that by means of these early paintings, Dogançay was able to resolve both his personal and his artistic quests in the prevailing atmosphere of the conflict betwen abstraction and realism. For example, for a period of time he painted on three-dimensional doors. These doors, locked, messy, and uninviting, spelled out appealing messages of hope, promises of entertainment, merriment, food, and love—all things from which the observer is barred, knowing that these are really illusory images and that nothing exists on the other side of the door.

At this point we saw an important change in Dogançay's work as he began to emerge from the artist as observer to the artist as speaker. The walls became blank, black, or white, symbolic of light and shade. Reality was no longer the surface, but that which lay behind it: elements from inside the wall burst forth, invading our space.

Previously, when his role was that of the observer, his compositions were fragmented and objects moved off beyond the limits of the picture. They were images of incomplete worlds, covering the whole picture space. When he became concerned with personal expression, however, his composition became centralized,

PRINCE MACARONI, 1965
Oil, collage and crayon on canvas, 30 × 40 ins. (76.2 × 101.6 cm.)

GENTIL INC., 1965
Oil on canvas, 30 × 24 ins. (76.2 × 61 cm.)

advancing toward the viewer rather than moving laterally, and his main image took on a Byzantine frontality, with large spaces between the activity of the painting and the frame. These compositions represent emotion controlled, isolated by a calming ground.

A significant phase in Doğançay's development occurred in the early 1970s, after he began making lithographs at Tamarind. Partly because of the medium itself, he relinquished his casual or found compositions and began to organize his paintings graphically, with flatter areas and brighter colors. These are works without irony, displaying a respite from emotion. During this time he gradually became aware of new possibilities in color and composition and concentrated on a nonobjective elegance. From this important experience he was able to resolve his conflict between subject and method, and the works of this period clearly lead to his most recent work.

When, in 1985, he began to experiment with colored backgrounds (grays, browns, blues, violets, and purples) his paintings took on an added richness. His images had formerly existed in an endless space of black or white. But, with the addition of color in the ground, the edges of the canvas became more defined, and as a consequence his composition changed. He was no longer working with the image in relationship to the tensions produced by the edges of the canvas.

So his shadows became longer, more diagonal, more dramatic, and more prominent. Because the color changed the background into object, the viewer now had

WATER SHORTAGE, 1965
Oil and collage on canvas,
30 × 24 ins. (76.2 × 61 cm.)

MADISON AVENUE, 1966
Collage and mixed media on tin, 24 × 36 ins. (61 × 91.4 cm.)

LOCKED UP, 1965
Oil and collage on canvas, 30 × 24 ins. (76.2 × 61 cm.)
Private collection, Paris

EDDIE, 1965
Gouache on cardboard, 28 × 28 ins. (71.1 × 71.1 cm.)

a field of reference in which the small subject casting larger shadows made the scale seem monumental. The light in some of these paintings comes from the left, producing long distorted shadows, reminding one of the fleeting light of late afternoon when changing light is more perceptible. This activates the canvas in a new and different way.

The hued ribbons are colored on the outside and white on the inside. This means that Dogançay is no longer experimenting with an image lying flat on the ground. He employs the most complex type of perspective conceivable on a two-dimensional surface: white (which advances toward the viewer) is now used for the *back* side of the ribbons which should visibly recede; primary color (which establishes the middle ground) is now used for the *front* of the ribbon which should advance toward the viewer; and black (which recedes) is now used to lie in the middle ground as a shadow on top of a color.

To put these topsy-turvy and contradictory elements together into a convincing three-dimensional image is miraculous. To do it without resorting to texture or impasto or brushstroke is even more ingenious, for Dogançay manages to maintain a cool, even, undifferentiated surface, which emphasizes the violent, chaotic, ambiguous subject content. His reduction of color to reds and yellows in the ribbons creates a hot, energetic image against the foil of a cool, grayed background.

NO. 2 WALL: FREE AGAIN, 1966
Oil, collage and mixed media on canvas, 60 × 80 ins. (152.4 × 203.2 cm.)
Collection Georgia Museum of Art, Athens, Georgia

Throughout his career Dogançay has been concerned with a tactile picture plane, from which the objects project into the space of the viewer.

Every artist paints his own concept of reality. Every artist knows that painting itself is an abstraction. To resolve realism and abstraction has been a special concern of artists in the post-abstract-expressionist period. But Dogançay never abandoned realism. He simply adapted it to an abstract format, which he invented as an expression of his own compelling emotions. He previously expressed his feelings vicariously through other people's messages. His new desire to reveal personal intensity, to expose his feelings, takes the extraordinary form of literally pouring out his insides to the viewer. The bright colors are heated emotional equivalents of sounds bursting through an unemotional facade.

In these new works, the interior expression spills out in a linear form of abstract script, thin strips or bands resembling cursive calligraphy. He thus returns once again to his earlier concept of the picture as writing. His message is now deliberately obscure, even mysterious, although intense. Like script, which reveals the hidden truth, Dogançay's new form of writing transforms his inner expression into a spiritual one, bridging the gap between painting and the word.

Dogançay now makes the world visible through shadows of strange words that are fleeting, transient, and dissolving. He has combined abstraction with realism by literally painting abstract shapes related to writing, the most abstract of all graphic images, further abstracted in Dogançay's paintings by the absence of verbal meaning.

As we contemplate the works of Dogançay with their ability to evoke joy, irony, love, humor, disappointment, vanity, or beauty, we come to realize that he has shown us ourselves as part of the human race at its best and its worst, and we learn what it means to be a human being.

ROY MOYER

ANTIQUES, 1965
Oil and mixed media on canvas, 80 × 80 ins. (203.2 × 203.2 cm.)

BARBRA, 1965
Oil and collage on canvas, 30 × 24 ins. (76.2 × 61 cm.)

BOBBY, 1965
Gouache and collage on cardboard, 30 × 24 ins. (76.2 × 61 cm.)

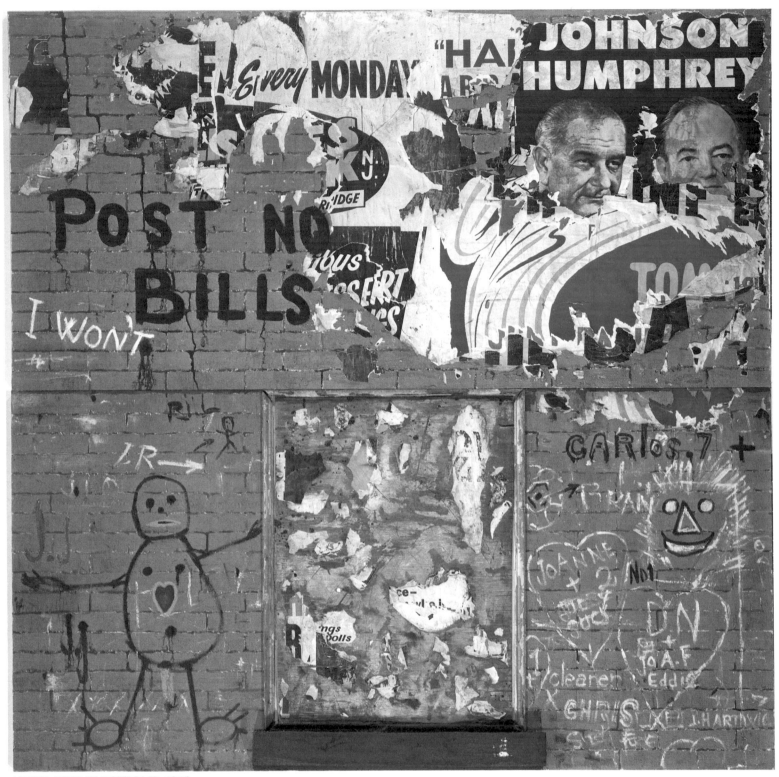

AFTER THE ELECTIONS, 1965
Oil and mixed media on canvas, 80 × 80 ins. (203.2 × 203.2 cm.)

RED OLD DOOR, 1965
Gouache on paper, 10 × 8 ins. (25.4 × 20.3 cm.)
Private collection, Istanbul

PINK DOOR, 1966
Oil, collage and mixed media on canvas, 59 × 32 ins. (149.9 × 81.3 cm.)

YELLOW DOOR, 1966
Oil, collage and mixed media on canvas, 59 × 32 ins. (149.9 × 81.3 cm.)
Private collection, Duisburg

TEEN A GO-GO, 1966
Oil and mixed media on canvas, 40 × 30 ins. (101.6 × 76.2 cm.)

DETERIORATION, 1966
Oil and collage on canvas, 60 × 80 ins. (152.4 × 203.2 cm.)

FIRST CLASS, 1966
Oil and mixed media on canvas, 80 × 40 ins. (203.2 × 101.6 cm.)

DAY AND NIGHT, 1966
Oil and mixed media on canvas, 80 × 60 ins. (203.2 × 152.4 cm.)

CHIPPED WALL, 1966
Oil on canvas, 48 × 48 ins. (122 × 122 cm.)

OFF, 1966
Oil and mixed media on canvas and Masonite, 48 × 80 ins. (122 × 203.2 cm.)
Collection The Snite Museum of Art, Notre Dame, Indiana

DETOUR, 1966
Oil and mixed media on canvas, 48 × 48 ins. (122 × 122 cm.)
Private collection, Dusseldorf

THE CHANGING SCENE OF NEW YORK, 1966
Oil and collage on cardboard, 30 × 23 ins. (76.2 × 58.4 cm.)

PEELED OFF, 1967
Oil on canvas, 40 × 40 ins. (101.6 × 101.6 cm.)

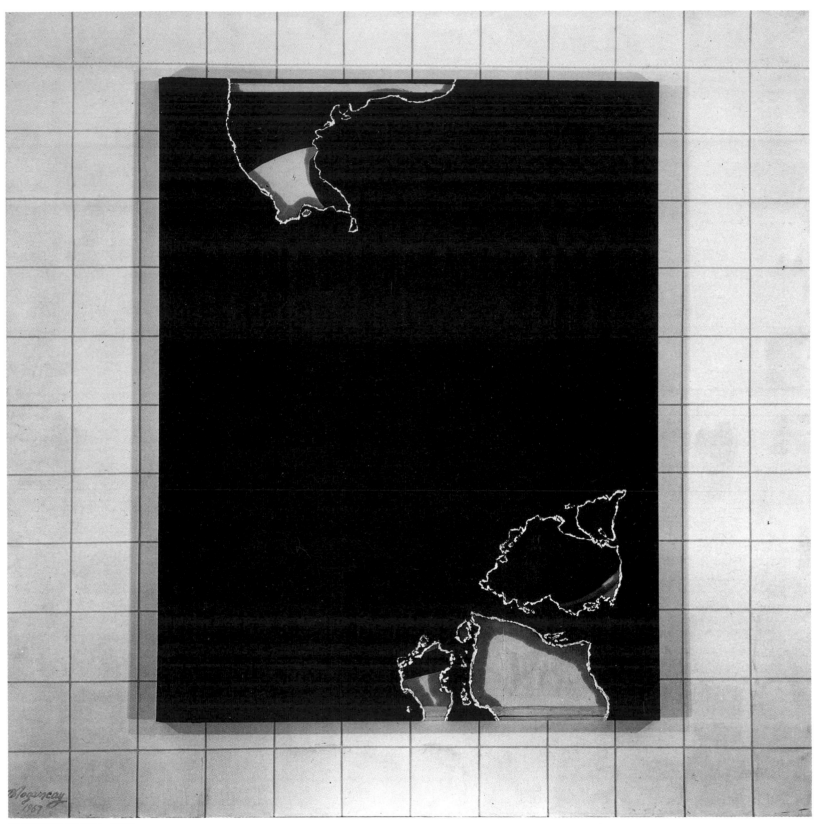

SUBWAY WALL, 1967
Oil and collage on canvas, 60 × 60 ins. (152.4 × 152.4 cm.)

JIGSAW PUZZLE, 1968
Gouache on paper, 22 × 24 ins. (55.9 × 61 cm.)

ABOLAFIA FOR MAYOR, 1968
Gouache and collage on paper, 9 × 10½ ins. (22.9 × 26.7 cm.)
Private collection, Dusseldorf

LOVE, 1969
Gouache, crayon and India ink on paper, 14½ × 10½ ins. (36.8 × 26.7 cm.)
Private collection, Istanbul

POSTERSCAPE, 1969
Gouache on paper, 30 × 22 ins. (76.2 × 55.9 cm.)

WALLS V, 1969
Lithograph, 24 × 19½ ins. (61 × 49.5 cm.), edition of 14
Published by Tamarind Lithography Workshop, Inc., Los Angeles

WALLS V, 1969
Lithograph, 23 × 19½ ins. (58.4 × 49.5 cm.), edition of 20
Published by Tamarind Lithography Workshop, Inc., Los Angeles

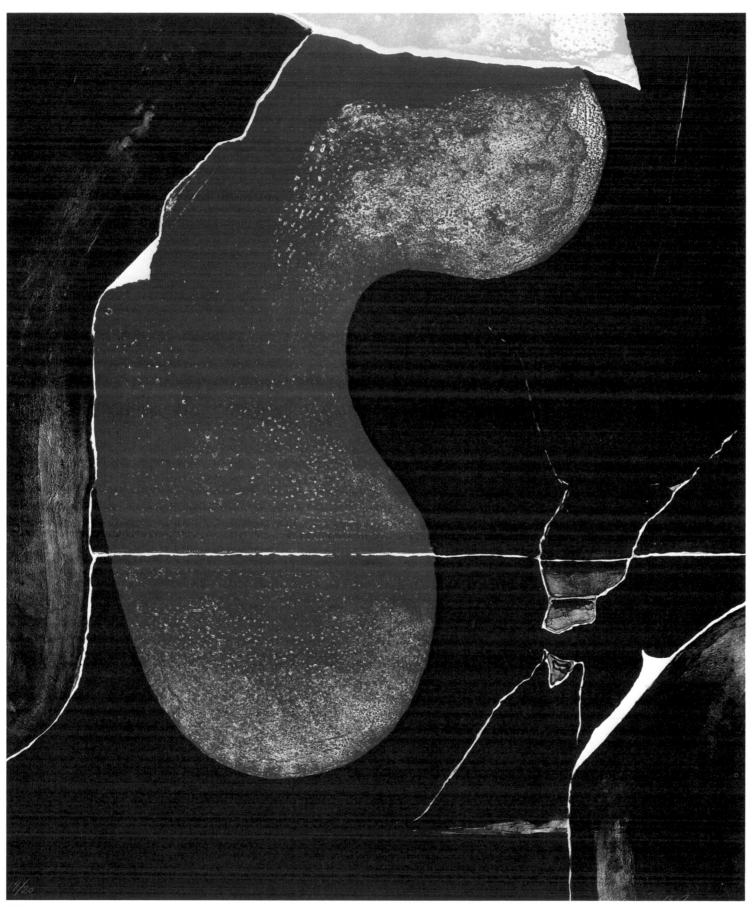

WALLS V, 1969
Lithograph, 23 × 19½ ins. (58.4 × 49.5 cm.), edition of 20
Published by Tamarind Lithography Workshop, Inc., Los Angeles

WALLS V, 1969
Lithograph, 23 × 19½ ins. (58.4 × 49.5 cm.), edition of 20
Published by Tamarind Lithography Workshop, Inc., Los Angeles

WALLS V, 1969
Lithograph, 23 × 19½ ins. (58.4 × 49.5 cm.), edition of 20
Published by Tamarind Lithography Workshop, Inc., Los Angeles

WALLS V, 1969
Lithograph, 23 × 19½ ins. (58.4 × 49.5 cm.), edition of 10
Published by Tamarind Lithography Workshop, Inc., Los Angeles

WALLS 70, 1970
Lithograph, 29½ × 22 ins. (74.9 × 55.9 cm.), edition of 120
Co-published by Bank Street Atelier, New York

WALLS 70, 1970
Lithograph, 29½ × 22 ins. (74.9 × 55.9 cm.), edition of 120
Co-published by Bank Street Atelier, New York

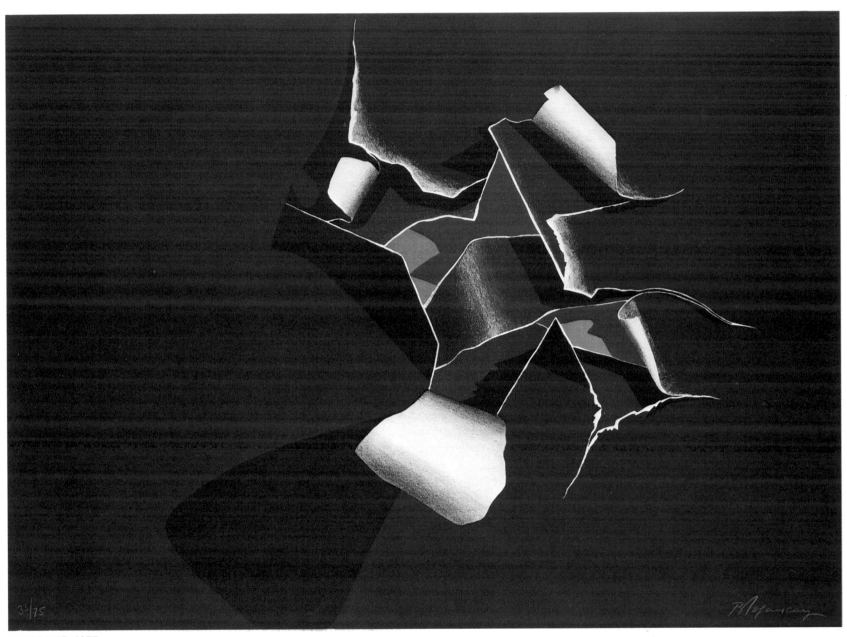

33/75

WALLS 77, 1977
Lithograph, 18¼ × 24½ ins. (46.4 × 62.2 cm.), edition of 75
Co-published by Atelier Wolfensberger, Zurich

FROM WALLS 70: No.8, 1970
Oil on canvas, 60 × 60 ins. (152.4 × 152.4 cm.)
Private collection, Duisburg

THE BOYS IN THE BAND, 1970
Gouache and collage on paper, 30 × 23 ins. (76.2 × 58.4 cm.)

FROM WALLS 70: No. 45, 1970
Acrylic on canvas, 60 × 60 ins. (152.4 × 152.4 cm.)

U AS IN SUGAR, 1970
Oil on canvas, 60 × 60 ins. (152.4 × 152.4 cm.)

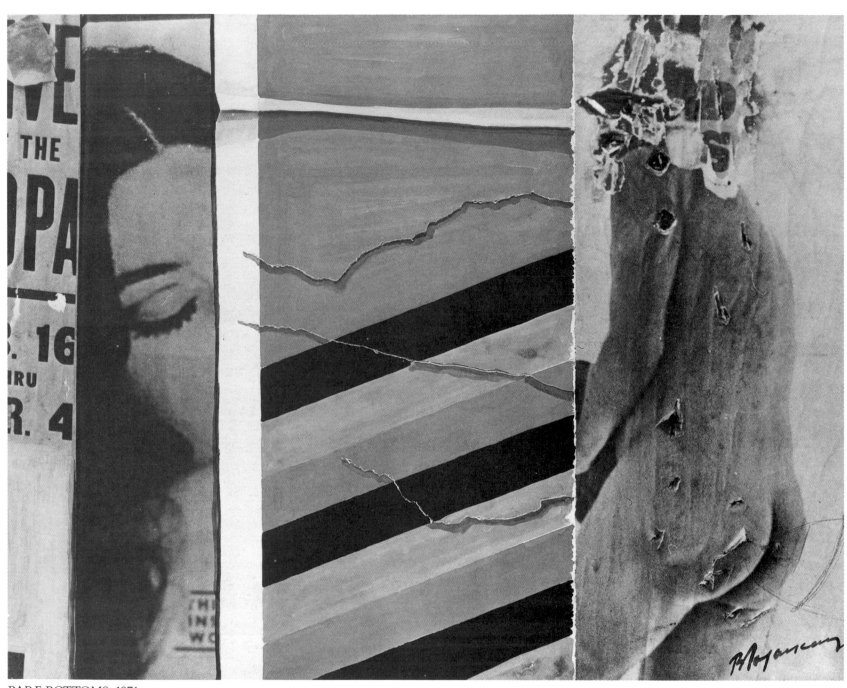

BARE BOTTOMS, 1971
Gouache and collage on paper, 23 × 30 ins. (58.4 × 76.2 cm.)

COMPOSITION: TORN POSTER, 1971
Acrylic on canvas, 60 × 50 ins. (152.4 × 127 cm.)
Private collection, Zurich

SIMPLY NO, 1971
Gouache on paper, 32 × 25 ins. (81.3 × 63.5 cm.)

BRICK WALL, 1971
Gouache on paper, 30 × 22 ins. (76.2 × 55.9 cm.)
Private collection, New York

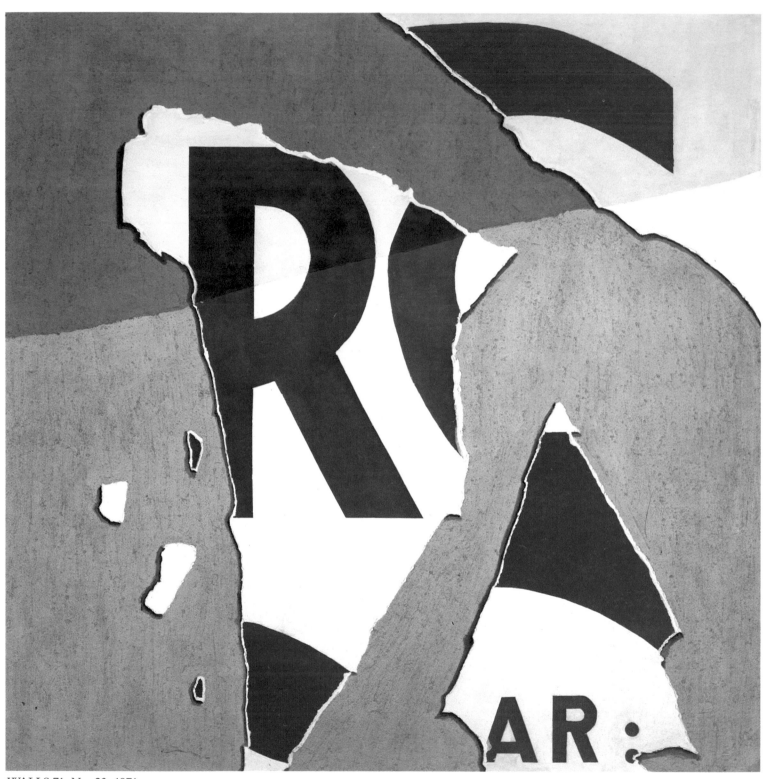

WALLS 71: No. 23, 1971
Oil on canvas, 60 × 60 ins. (152.4 × 152.4 cm.)
Private collection, Dusseldorf

SIX AND FIVE, 1972
Acrylic on canvas, 60 × 60 ins. (152.4 × 152.4 cm.)

COMPOSITION: BROKEN LETTERS, 1972
Acrylic on canvas, 50 × 50 ins. (127 × 127 cm.)
Collection Galerie Swidbert, Dusseldorf

SHADOWS ON A GRAY WALL, 1972
Oil on canvas, 60 × 60 ins. (152.4 × 152.4 cm.)

MY PRIVATE SPY, 1972
Acrylic on canvas, 60 × 60 ins. (152.4 × 152.4 cm.)
Collection Swarovski, Wattens, Austria

FIVE CENTS PLUS, 1972
Acrylic on canvas, 40 × 40 ins. (101.6 × 101.6 cm.)

A AS IN AMOUR I, 1972
Gouache on paper, 17 × 14 ins. (43.2 × 35.6 cm.)
Collection Galerie Swidbert, Dusseldorf

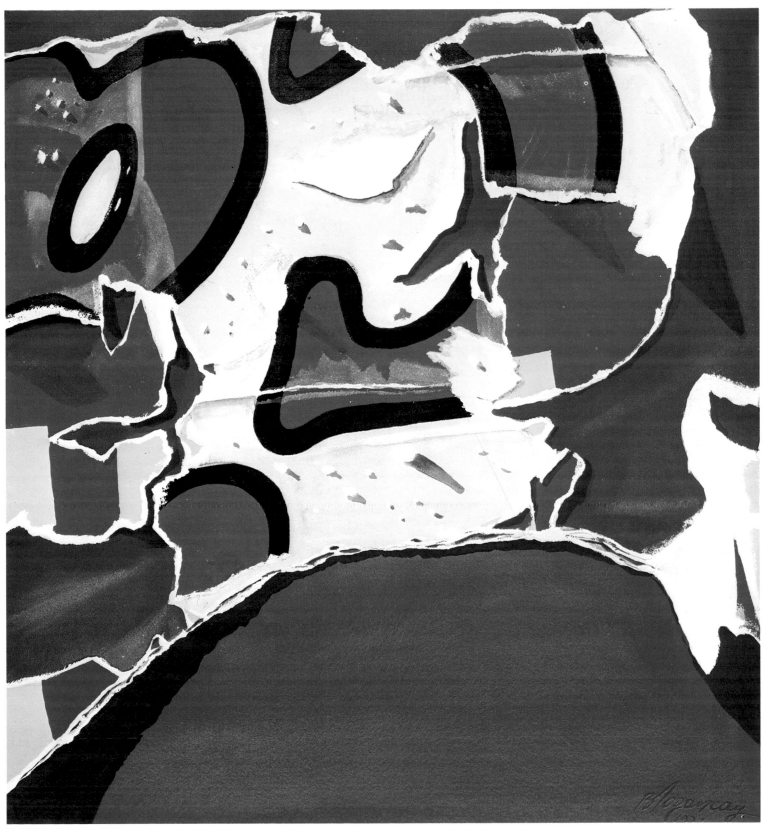

LIVELY COOL, 1972
Gouache on paper, 24 × 21¼ ins. (61 × 54 cm.)

TRIANGULAR SHADOWS ON YELLOW, 1972
Acrylic on canvas, 35 × 50 ins. (88.9 × 127 cm.)
Collection The Chase Manhattan Bank, N.A., New York

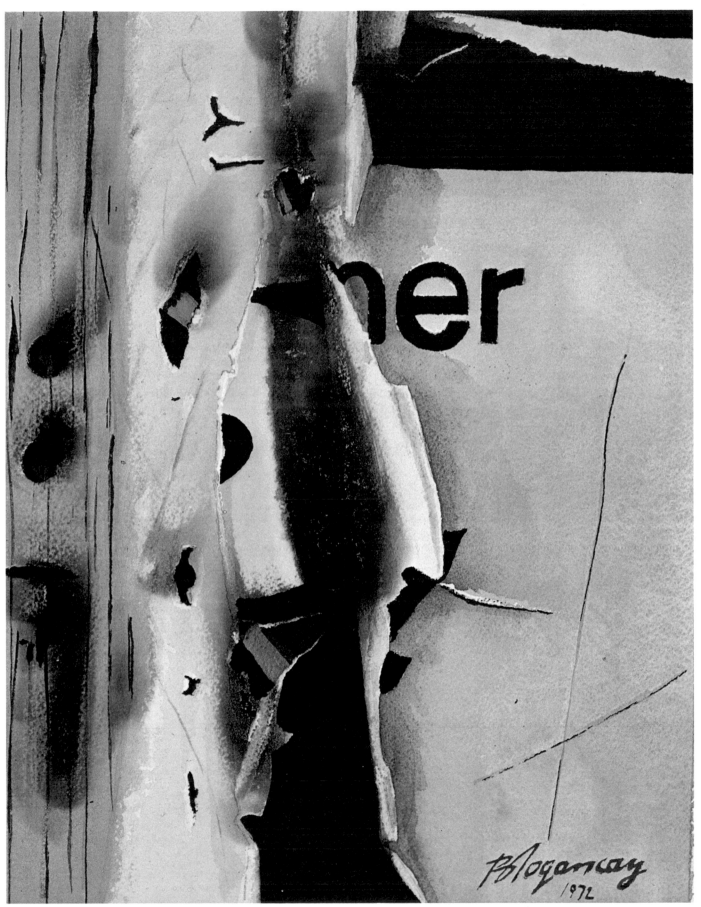

CORNER, 1972
Gouache and fumage on paper, 15 × 12 ins. (38.1 × 30.5 cm.)

IC AS IN TERRIFIC, 1972
Gouache and fumage on paper, 22 × 20 ins. (55.9 × 50.8 cm.)
Private collection, New York

MAGIC MOUNTAIN, 1972
Gouache on paper, 23 × 22½ ins. (58.4 × 57.2 cm.)
Collection Galerie Swidbert, Dusseldorf

SWEET HEARTS, 1972
Gouache on paper, 30 × 22 ins. (76.2 × 55.9 cm.)
Private collection, Paris

EMERGENCE, 1973
Gouache on paper, 16 × 12 ins. (40.6 × 30.5 cm.)
UNICEF card 1974

WAVE, 1973
Gouache on paper, 22½ × 22½ ins. (57.2 × 57.2 cm.)
Private collection, Berkeley Heights, New Jersey

LA GRANDE BOUFFE, 1973
Gouache, collage and fumage on paper, 13¾ × 11¼ ins. (35 × 28.6 cm.)
Private collection, New York

TURNING THE CORNER, 1973
Gouache and fumage on paper, 17½ × 17½ ins. (44.5 × 44.5 cm.)
Private collection, Paris

LETTER FRAGMENTATION, 1973
Gouache and fumage on paper, 11¾ × 11¾ ins. (30 × 30 cm.)

PM, 1973
Acrylic on canvas, 48 × 48 ins. (122 × 122 cm.)

BENDING OVER, 1973
Acrylic on canvas, 24 × 20 ins. (61 × 50.8 cm.)

COMPOSITION: YELLOW AND PINK, 1973
Gouache on paper, 17 × 17 ins. (43.2 × 43.2 cm.)

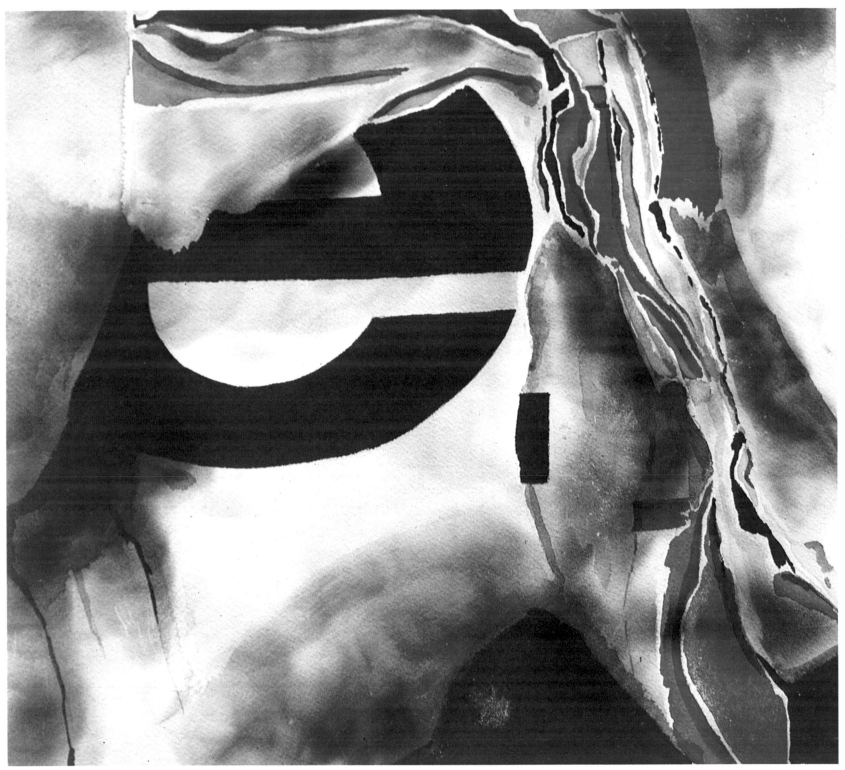

BIG SMALL E, 1973
Gouache and fumage on paper, 22 × 28 ins. (55.9 × 71.1 cm.)

X-RAY IN COLOR, 1973
Gouache and fumage on paper, 12 × 11 ins. (30.5 × 27.9 cm.)
Collection Galerie Swidbert, Dusseldorf

TORN RED AND BLACK PAPERS, 1974
Gouache on paper, 8 × 11½ ins. (20.3 × 29.2 cm.)

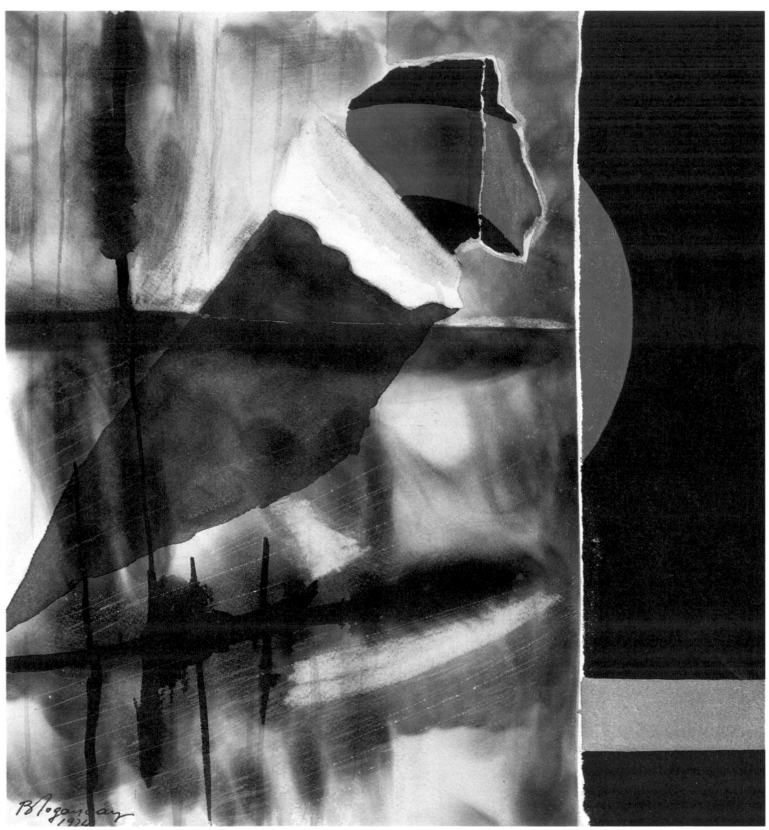

DUMANLI, 1974
Gouache and fumage on paper, 14 × 13 ins. (35.6 × 33 cm.)
Collection The Solomon R. Guggenheim Museum, New York

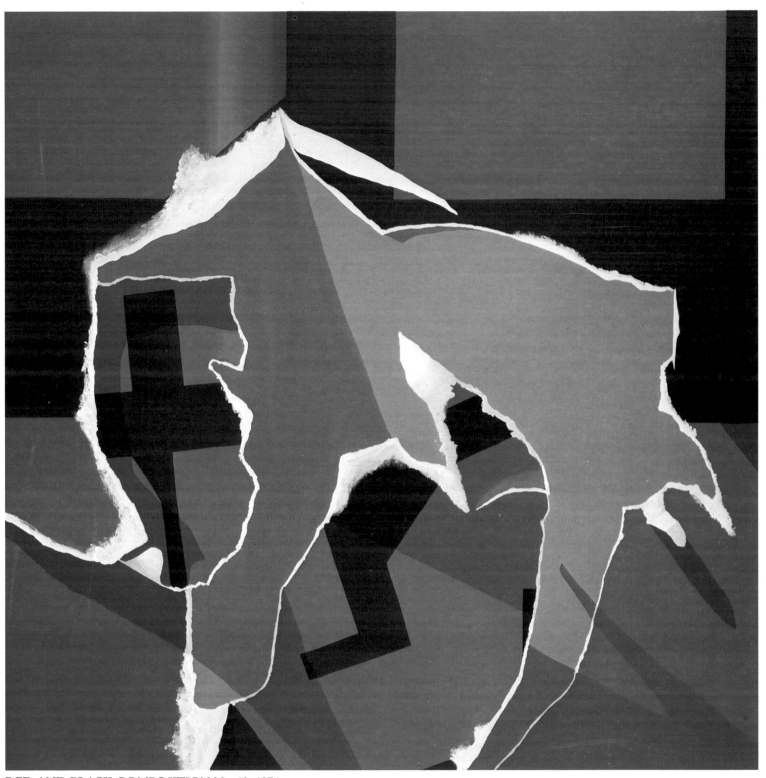

RED AND BLACK COMPOSITION No. 10, 1974
Acrylic on canvas, 60 × 60 ins. (152.4 × 152.4 cm.)
Private collection, Duisburg

RED AND BLACK COMPOSITION No. 5, 1974
Acrylic on canvas, 60 × 60 ins. (152.4 × 152.4 cm.)
Collection The Solomon R. Guggenheim Museum, New York

RISING SUN, 1974
Acrylic on canvas, 60 × 60 ins. (152.4 × 152.4 cm.)

ISLE, 1974
Gouache and fumage on paper, 14 × 11 ins. (35.6 × 27.9 cm.)
Collection The Solomon R. Guggenheim Museum, New York

SLINKY, 1975
Gouache and fumage on paper, 22 × 22 ins. (55.9 × 55.9 cm.)

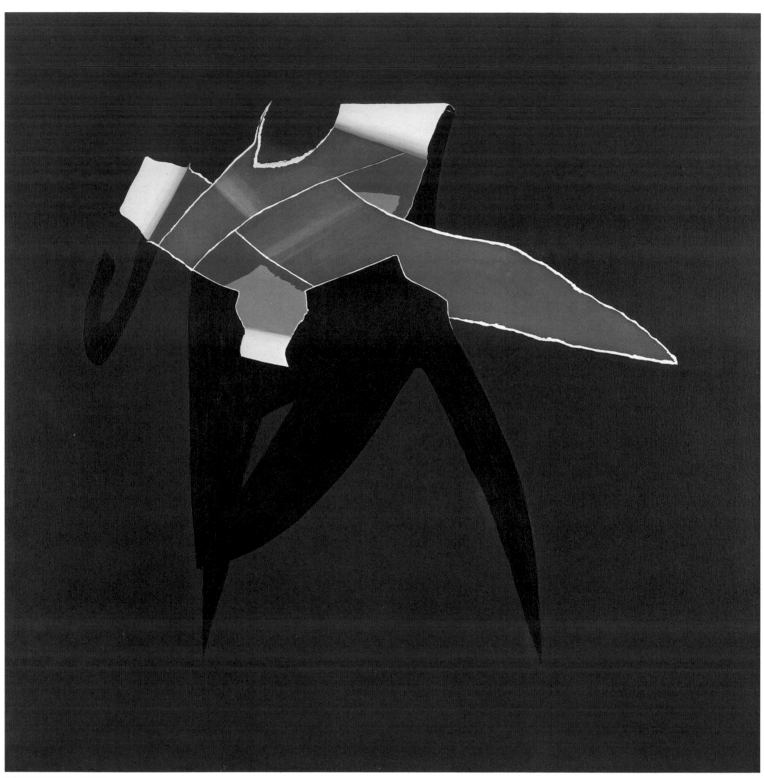

UNTITLED, 1975
Acrylic on canvas, 50 × 50 ins. (127 × 127 cm.)
Collection The Newark Museum, Newark, New Jersey

THE GREAT BREAKTHROUGH, 1976
Acrylic on canvas, 60 × 60 ins. (152.4 × 152.4 cm.)

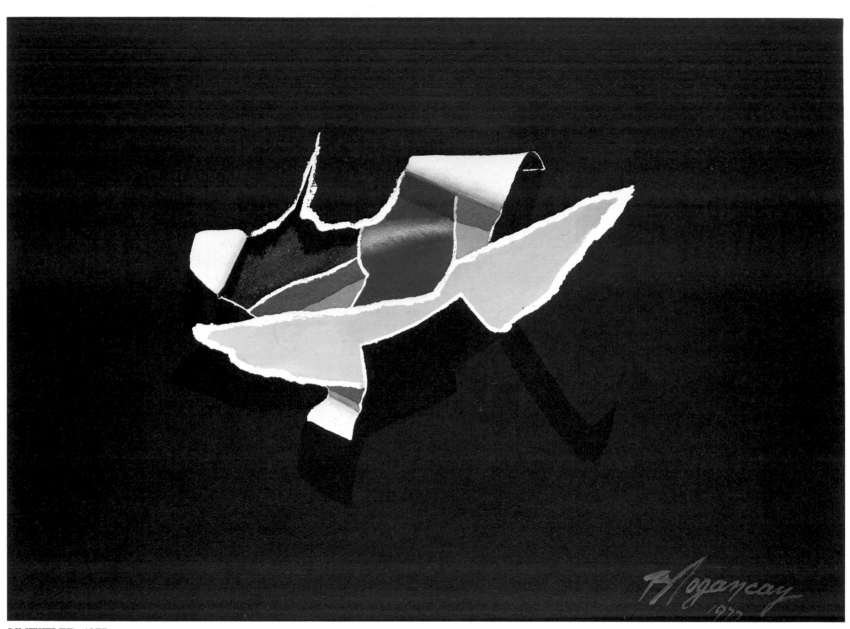

UNTITLED, 1977
Gouache on paper, 11¼ × 15 ins. (28.6 × 38.1 cm.)
Collection The Solomon R. Guggenheim Museum, New York

DEFENSE D'AFFICHER, 1977
Crayon on paper, 10 × 12 ins. (25.4 × 30.5 cm.)

WALLS OF PARIS, study, 1977
Gouache, crayon, collage and ink on paper, 10 × 12 ins. (25.4 × 30.5 cm.)

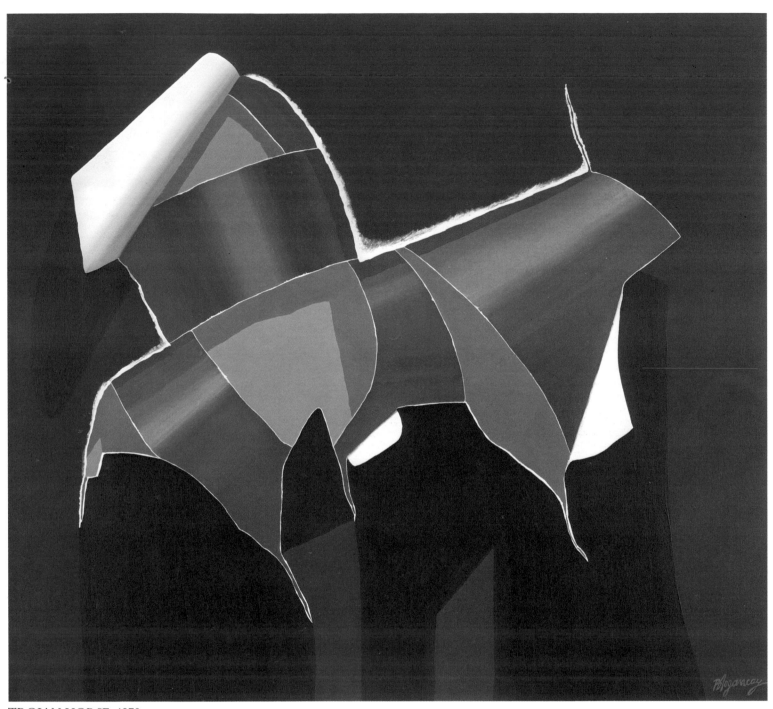

TROJAN HORSE ,1978
Acrylic on canvas, 60 × 66 ins. (152.4 × 167.6 cm.)

STRIPES AND SHADOWS, 1978
Acrylic on canvas, 60 × 60 ins. (152.4 × 152.4 cm.)

UNTITLED, 1978
Acrylic on canvas, 50 × 40 ins. (127 × 101.6 cm.)
Collection Michael C. Rockefeller Arts Center, Fredonia, New York

HOMAGE TO CALLIGRAPHY I, 1981
Acrylic on canvas, 60 × 60 ins. (152.4 × 152.4 cm.)

A LITTLE NIGHT MUSIC II, 1982
Acrylic on canvas, 60 × 60 ins. (152.4 × 152.4 cm.)
Private collection, Summit, New Jersey

ESCAPE I, 1982
Acrylic on canvas, 60 × 60 ins. (152.4 × 152.4 cm.)

DOUBLE PLEASURE, 1982
Gouache on paper, 18 × 26 ins. (45.7 × 66 cm.)
Private collection, New York

POINTED SHADOWS, 1983
Gouache on paper, 30 × 22 ins. (76.2 × 55.9 cm.)

UNTITLED, 1983
Wool tapestry, 59¾ × 44½ ins. (152 × 113 cm.)
Executed by L'Atelier Raymond Picaud, Aubusson

UNTITLED, 1983
Wool tapestry, 59¾ × 44½ ins. (152 × 113 cm.)
Executed by L'Atelier Raymond Picaud, Aubusson

PIROUETTE, 1983
Gouache on paper, 30 × 22 ins. (76.2 × 55.9 cm.)
Private collection, New York

UNTITLED, 1984
Gouache on paper, 30 × 22 ins. (76.2 × 55.9 cm.)
Private collection, New York

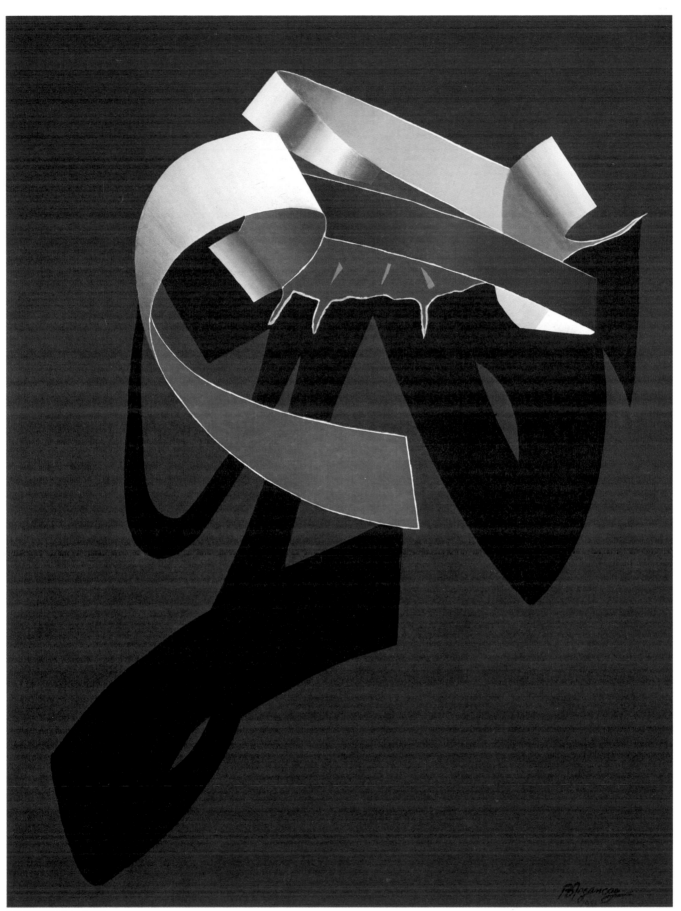

UNTITLED, 1984
Acrylic on canvas, 40 × 32 ins. (101.6 × 81.3 cm.)

UNTITLED, 1984
Acrylic on canvas, 32 × 40 ins. (81.3 × 101.6 cm.)

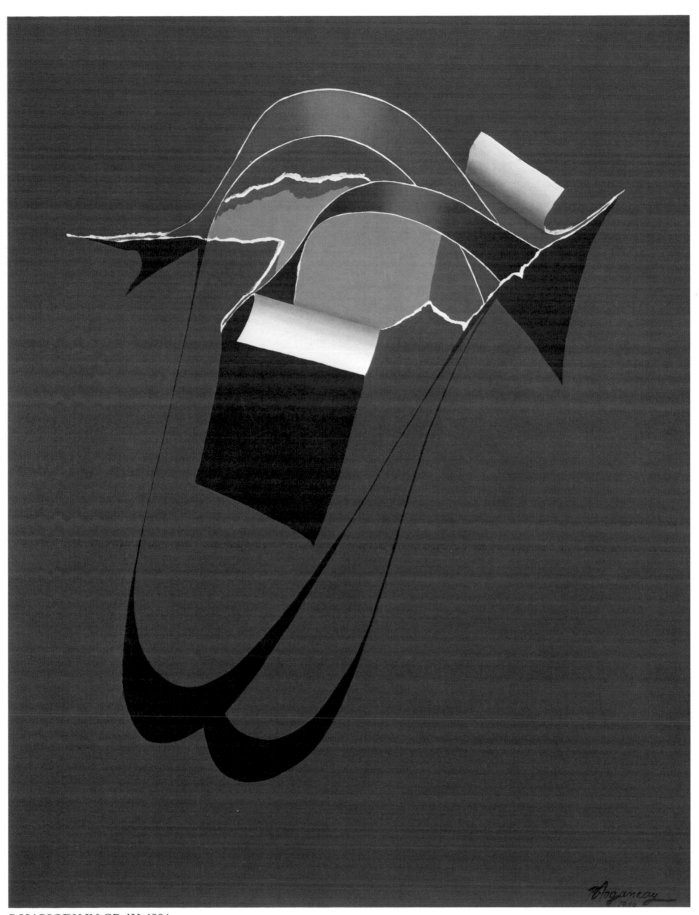

RHAPSODY IN GRAY, 1984
Acrylic on canvas, 40 × 31 ins. (101.6 × 78.7 cm.)

UNTITLED, 1984
Acrylic on canvas, 40 × 32 ins. (101.6 × 81.3 cm.)

BLACK AND YELLOW LOOPS, 1985
Acrylic on canvas, 40 × 30 ins. (101.6 × 76.2 cm.)

BLOSSOM, 1985
Acrylic on canvas, 50 × 36 ins. (127 × 91.4 cm.)

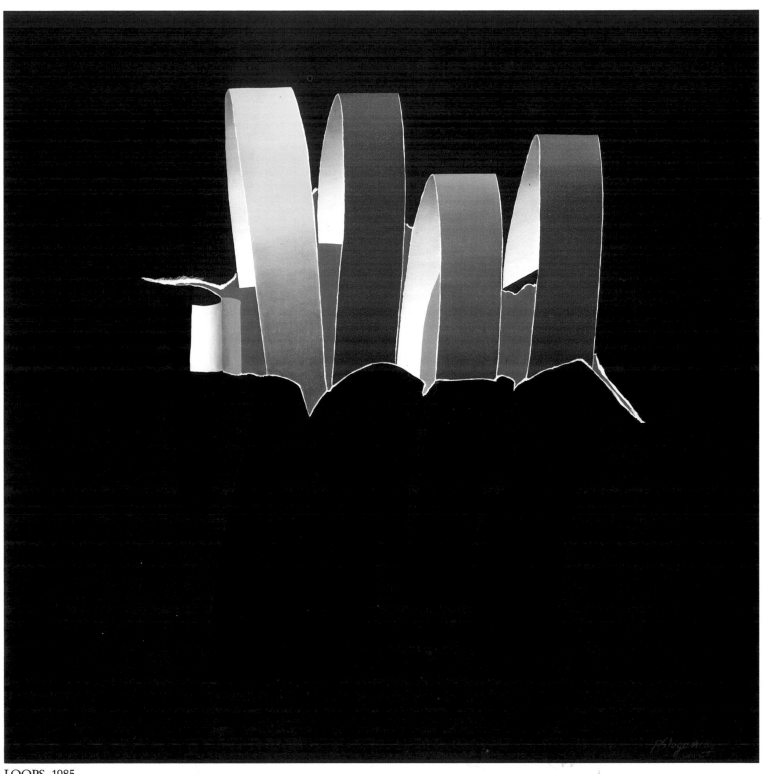

LOOPS, 1985
Acrylic on canvas, 40 × 40 ins. (101.6 × 101.6 cm.)

UNTITLED, 1985
Acrylic on canvas, 40 × 40 ins. (101.6 × 101.6 cm.)

UNTITLED, 1985
Acrylic on canvas, 50 × 36 ins. (127 × 91.4 cm.)

HOMAGE TO CALLIGRAPHY II, 1985
Acrylic on canvas, 40 × 40 ins. (101.6 × 101.6 cm.)
Private collection, New York

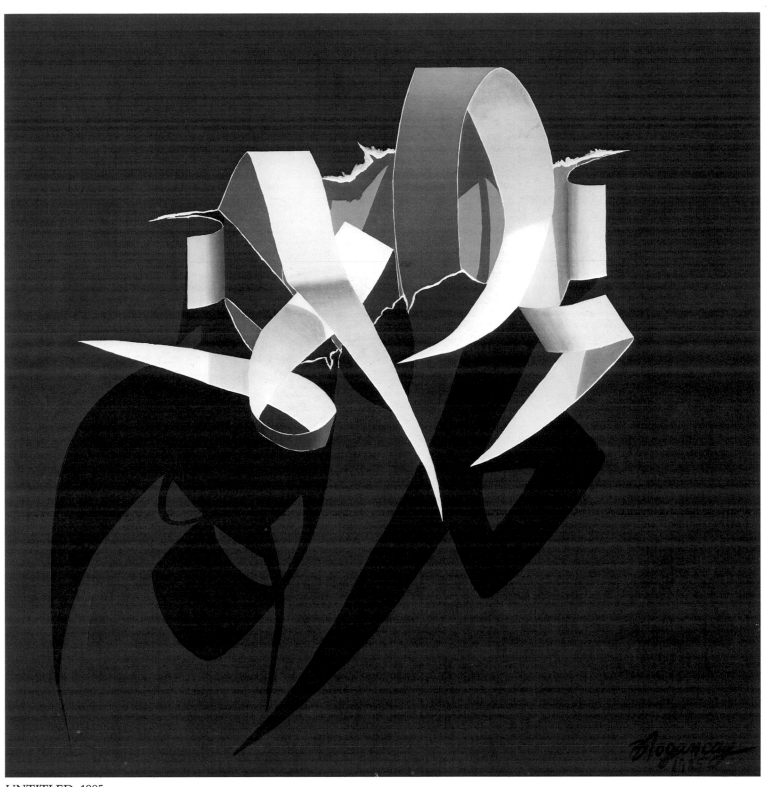

UNTITLED, 1985
Acrylic on canvas, 40 × 40 ins. (101.6 × 101.6 cm.)

UNTITLED, 1985
Acrylic on canvas, 36 × 50 ins. (91.4 × 127 cm.)

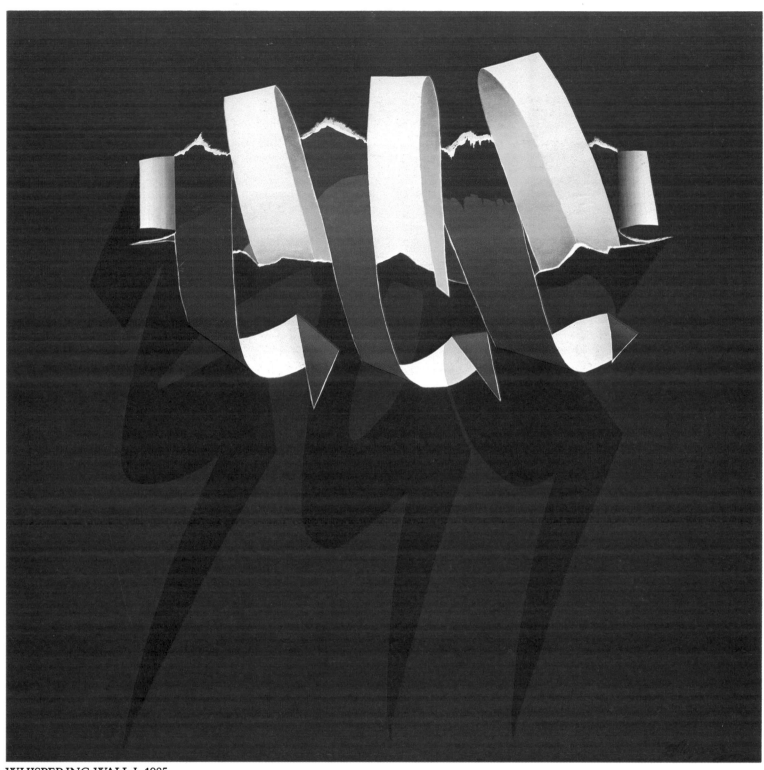

WHISPERING WALL I, 1985
Acrylic on canvas, 52 × 52 ins. (132.1 × 132.1 cm.)

LE ROUGE ET LE NOIR, 1985
Acrylic on canvas, 48 × 71 ins. (122 × 180.3 cm.)

WHISPERING WALL II, 1985
Acrylic on canvas, 52 × 72 ins. (132.1 × 182.9 cm.)

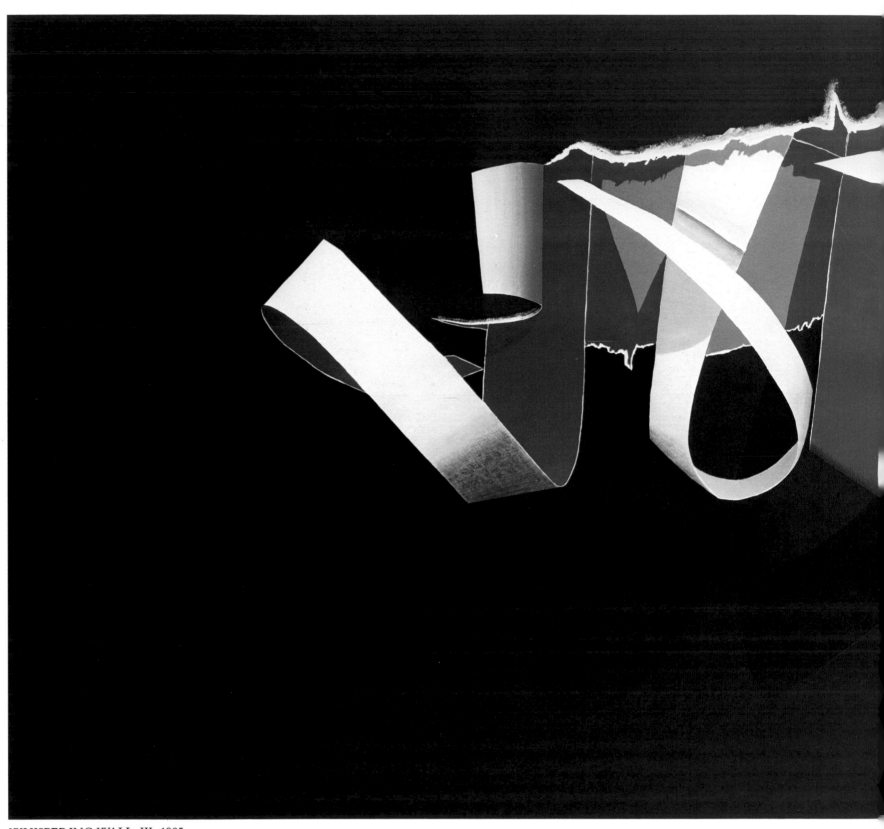

WHISPERING WALL III, 1985
Acrylic on canvas, 40 × 90 ins. (101.6 × 228.6 cm.)

SHADOW

SCULPTURE

The first picture was a single line drawn round the shadow of a man cast by the sun on the wall.

—LEONARDO DA VINCI

All of Doğançay's works show a battle for volume that is most fully realized in his sculpture.

The evolution of his sculpture, generated by his inner growth, parallels the historical development of classical Greek sculpture, from painting to low-relief, to high-relief, to sculpture completely in the round. Since the image against a ground can only be viewed frontally, Doğançay's three-dimensional sculpture must be seen as contiguous facades of a polygon.

The bands of color, which project from the background, define varying areas of space. The spaces enclosed by the bands therefore have degrees of density; and the sculptor develops his composition by arranging pools of varying densities of air.

To consider air and space as something positive and manipulable, as elements to be composed as one would compose from stone or clay, is imaginable only in an age when air and space travel have confirmed this concept. Doğançay's sculpture does not lie inert, surrounded by space. It embraces the space, reaches out for it, and binds itself to it.

These bands, which bind, are of differing strengths: black bands like bands of iron; yellow bands like frivolous ribbons. They push from behind the wall with their pure white underbellies and burst into color when exposed to light: a photosynthesis like the green of the leaf and the blush on the rose.

When Doğançay paints, he first makes an actual three-dimensional model, lights it to emphasize the volume, and studies it like a still life. It is natural that his sculpture, derived from these models, would eventually become an independent art form.

As a child in Turkey, Doğançay learned to identify the shadow of an object with the spirit. From childhood he watched the shadow puppets of the traveling *Karagöz* troupes and saw that the shadows are expressive essences capable of expanding and contracting, transforming into giants or disappearing in a flash. It is not difficult to see this as a metaphor for life itself, for the haunting mystery of elusive and transient spirits.

We are not accustomed to recognizing shadows as a part of something. When we describe an object, we never mention shadows. But the sculpture of Doğançay gives equal value to object and shadow. So the artist has not simply introduced a new element of *immediate time* into his art (watching the shadows move is like watching the image being created), he has also moved from the illusionism of painting to the reality of tangible sculpture by taking the background of his paintings along with him into his sculpture. His shadows move across the flat surface: a form of painting in process, shifting form created by light. Shadows become substance, and background becomes object. The shadows are alive, in contrast to the physically still sculpture. His sculpture works to reveal the essence of our everyday space-time continuum. This gives it its own unique character. His forms emulate the energy of nature, twisting coils of tangled roots or interlacing branches. Each such shape explores the three dimensions of space-as-limitless-environment, and illustrates the continuity of time. He works with linear surfaces, developing them as functions of continually changing lines. Since they deliberately avoid visual stops, their total effect seems to be both fixed and writhing, definite and elusive, rigid and flaccid. This is the essential quality of nature.

Because the human body is permeated by the same energies that Dogançay's sculptures exude, they evoke intense sympathy. Dogançay's sculptures have a harmonizing influence, bringing the mental world of the viewer into direct relationship with the pattern of currents, in which nature is immersed. They remind us of our own constantly circulating physical and mental systems. The ribbons of energy in the sculpture are like the reins that harness our own sexual energies.

Dogançay studies the colors of shadows and their degrees of intensity. The color ground of his sculpture not only throws the projecting elements into a desired relationship, but also changes the color of shadows. And the depth of the sculpture creates a tonal value from darkest black to sheerest film, analogous to the shadows of the stalactite niches and ceilings of Turkish architecture.

Varying degrees of shadow and depth heighten the mystery and cause the wall to evaporate, emphasizing the insubstantial quality of materials. This shifting aspect of life is a constant theme of Dogançay's art in all its forms.

ROY MOYER

YELLOW TAIL, 1983
Alucobond and aluminum, 37½ × 26 ins. (95.3 × 66 cm.)

NATURA, 1983
Alucobond and oxidated, acidated aluminum, 46 × 80 ins. (116.8 × 203.2 cm.)

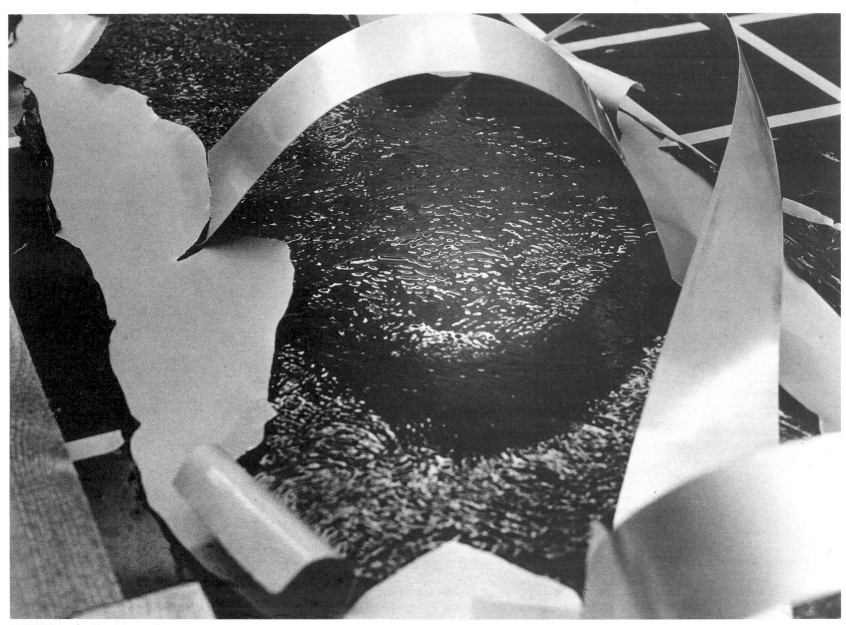

NATURA, detail while work in progress, 1983

CUBED SHADOW SCULPTURE, 1983
Alucobond and aluminum, motorized, 29 × 29 × 29 ins. (73.7 × 73.7 × 73.7 cm.)
Collection Swiss Aluminium Ltd., Zurich

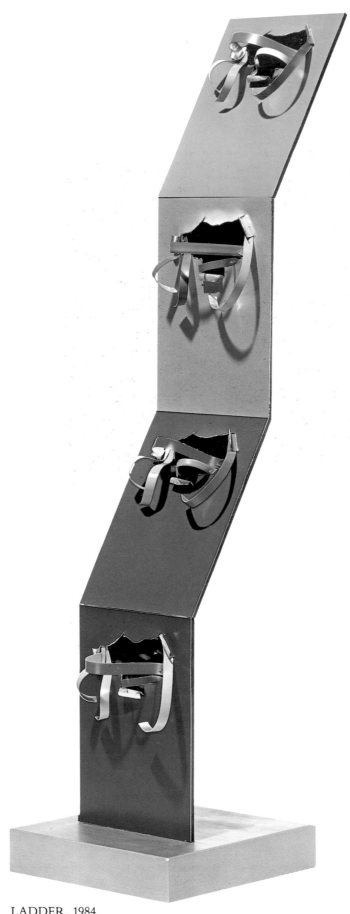

LADDER, 1984
Alucobond and aluminum, 22 × 4½ ins. (55.9 × 11.4 cm.)

TRIANGULAR COLUMN, 1984
Alucobond and aluminum, 11 × 7 × 7 ins. (27.9 × 17.8 × 17.8 cm.)

PYRAMID I, 1984
Alucobond and aluminum, 9 × 8 × 8 ins. (22.9 × 20.3 × 20.3 cm.)

Front

EQUILIBRIUM, 1984
Alucobond and aluminum, 6 × 13½ × 3 ins. (15.2 × 34.3 × 7.6 cm.)

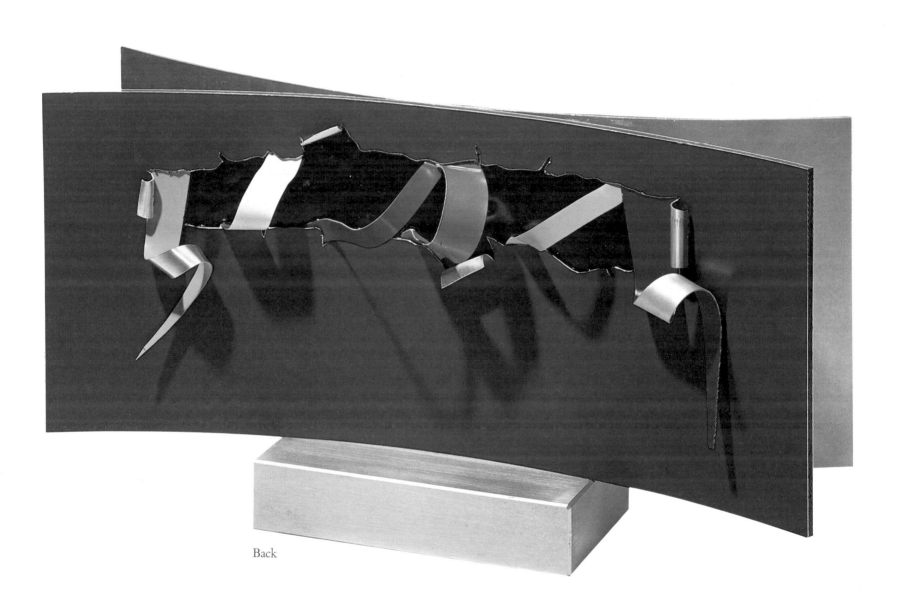

Back

179

VICTORY, 1984
Alucobond and aluminum, 11 × 7 × 5 ins. (27.9 × 17.8 × 12.7 cm.)

UNTITLED, 1984
Alucobond and aluminum, 8 × 8 ins. (20.3 × 20.3 cm.)

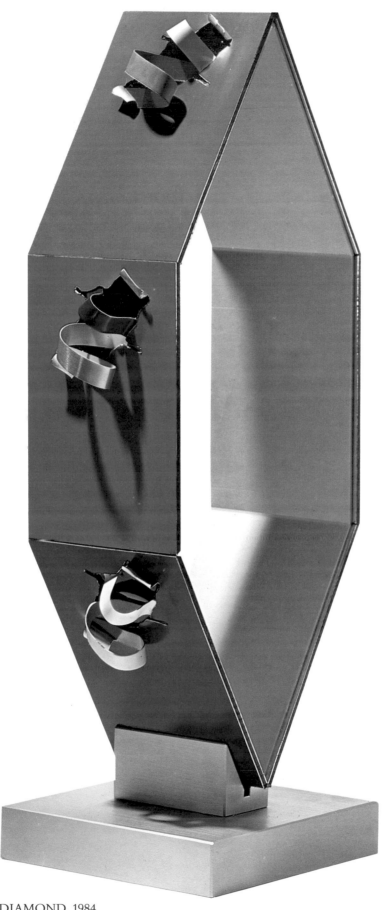

DIAMOND, 1984
Alucobond and aluminum, 17 × 4⅛ × 6½ ins. (43.2 × 10.5 × 16.5 cm.)

Front

CONCAVE SHADOW SCULPTURE, 1984 – Alucobond and aluminum, 11 × 6 × 3 ins. (27.9 × 15.2 × 7.6 cm.)

Back

PHOTOGRAPHY —

WALLS of the WORLD

You can read the pulse of a country by looking at its walls. —BURHAN DOGANÇAY

The Archives of the City

On the walls of cities, posters are put up, slashed, covered by other posters, or ripped off by the wind and rain. In big letters or small, city-dwellers tell their loves, write down their hatreds, affirm their convictions, or confess their doubts. Writing is mixed with drawings—some fairly primitive, some quite complex—and with paintings, too, some of which are naive, some accomplished.

Figures and texts on walls sometimes last, remaining there for years. Sometimes they only last an hour. They are the paradoxically short-lived archives of urban life, the annals of individual and collective passions that spring up and disappear in the city. They are the testimony, often neglected or treated with contempt, of the emotional ebb and flow that pulses through the city and the hearts of its inhabitants. Many people do not look at them, do not read them, do not decipher them. They refuse to consider them as anything but a stain. Others, on the contrary—and in particular, the painter and photographer Burhan Dogançay—turn themselves into readers of walls, responsive to messages from unknown people, eager to welcome them and preserve them.

For nearly twenty years, Dogançay has been roaming through the world with his camera in his hand. He already has over twelve thousand slides—some twelve thousand documents of graffiti, posters, and other wall markings. This is doubtless the only such collection in the world. Dogançay has made himself an archivist of the hum of city life, the archaeologist of its emotions, the witness of the sighs and spells of anger that sweep through the most varied cities.

He is constantly on the alert for whatever is traced on fences, half-ruined houses, or rich homes. Like a hunter, he must constantly be attentive, constantly prepared to "trap" things that may disappear in a flash. He walks, he strolls through the jungle that is every city. But his strolling has a purpose. His walks through the world's cities combine nonchalance and intense attention. He dreams about the city the better to perceive it. He is guided by a kind of intuition. "The main thing," he says, "is to arrive at the right moment. You must be ready to pin down an image instantly, because you rarely ever get a second chance."

It is impossible to put off the recording of a wall message until tomorrow. It is impossible to postpone the time when the report is filed. "Coming back to the same spot," he adds, "a few days or even a few hours later means taking

LES MURS MURMURENT, ILS CRIENT, ILS CHANTENT. . . , 1982
Exhibition poster, 28 × 20 ins. (71.1 × 50.8 cm.), designed by Garth Bell for
Centre de Création Industrielle, Centre Georges Pompidou, Paris

the chance of seeing the wall demolished, the writing changed, or the whole thing completely erased."

At the same time Dogançay records the emotions of the city, he enables us to see the precariousness of its messages, the rapid changes that transform the city: walls that crumble, faces famous one day and obscure a few months later, changes on the surfaces of the walls.

"You do not cross the same river twice," said Heraclitus in a well-known phrase. From the pictures Dogançay has taken in Athens, Paris, Montreal and Jerusalem, one could paraphrase and say that you do not walk twice along the same street, you do not spend two evenings in the same town.

Every city dweller, whether he is aware of it or not, is a nomad, wandering along unstable walls, around perpetually changing surfaces, while the passions and ways of life of men and women are also being utterly transformed.

Paper Often Lasts Longer Than Stone

Thus, the photographer's experience emphasizes a few truisms that are all too often forgotten. For here we can see that paper is more solid, more permanent than stone. The hardness of walls, their massive character, makes them more fragile, more ephemeral in the end than the sheet of paper on which their message is recorded by the photographer.

In a sense, the photographer fulfills the wish of the person who writes on a wall, even while he modifies the writer's message. What was quickly sketched out with a brush or a spray can is recorded by a machine. What was meant to be read from afar on a vertical wall can now be looked at close up in a book lying horizontal on a table.

At the same time, the photographer makes it possible for different times and spaces to come together. A heart drawn in Montreal in 1981 can be juxtaposed with a heart painted in Jerusalem in 1972, the glasses of a Parisian politician placed next to the eyebrows of a Soviet ruler. The smile of a left-wing Belgian can be compared to the smile of a right-wing American.

The Photographer as Detective

Often this photographer of walls acts as a detective. He is the one who uncovers things, who reveals. But oddly enough he uncovers just what is displayed on the surface. He obliges us to see what was hidden from no one, but forgotten by everyone. On their surfaces, walls bear political messages that pollsters vainly

Montreal

Tel Aviv

Jerusalem

Montreal

struggle to translate. With greater precision and violence than sociologists, walls speak of the desires and anxieties of men and women; they whisper them or shout them in letters two yards high, but no one—or almost no one—hears.

Often what happens to walls is what happens to the purloined letter in Edgar Allan Poe's tale. It is precisely because the message is obvious that many people fail to perceive it. In Poe's tale, the wicked minister conceals the stolen letter by refusing to hide it, by leaving it in the open, on a card tray among some visiting cards. In the same way, the unconscious of the city is concealed—quite involuntarily —by standing right in the public eye. Dogançay is like Poe's hero Dupin. He examines what others neglect because they think they have already seen it. He reveals what they do not know—exactly because they think they have already learned it. His photographs isolate fragments of walls and thus oblige the viewer to perceive what the mass of the city's walls prevented him from seeing. Each photograph focuses the eye on a confined space, making it easier for the viewer to explore. It makes us look more attentively, more sharply. It divides the surface of the wall *differently*. It reframes it. It organizes the surface, helps us to grasp it.

A foreigner in the cities through which he roams, Dogançay has the advantage of a man who is easily surprised, a man with an unjaded eye. He has a fresh way of seeing, and perceives things that a sedentary person has stopped looking at. Dogançay's mobility enables him to deepen his knowledge of the city. He does not live there, he does not settle down. But he is—more than the ordinary inhabitants of the city—sensitive to what is registered there, to things in the inhabitants they did not know about themselves. An ethnologist of urban societies, an unlicensed psychoanalyst, the wall photographer likes to be close to—and distant from—what he photographs. He loves each city and leaves it for another. He is a wanderer who knows what the inhabitant feels, thinks, invents, better than does the inhabitant himself.

He takes his pictures in passing, sometimes on the sly. Then he works from them to reconstruct the face of a nation or a city. "Graffiti, philosophical and political slogans, children's drawings, and funny, tragic, or erotic writings all reveal," says Dogançay, "the social, political, economic, cultural and commercial personality of a country, a city, or a town." But this revelation is ignored, it is opaque and impenetrable before the foreign observer comes in—a man with a camera.

The Tender Heart

The photographer can show that tenderness is present in cities at least as frequently as hatred or crude desire. Often people are more ashamed of their tender-

Lisbon

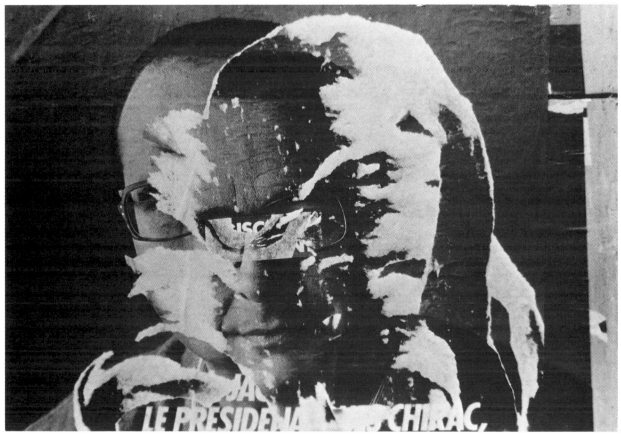

Paris

Cairo

ness than of their violence. They confess their tenderness furtively, often anonymously. They hide in order to say they love and they would like to be loved. They scream, hiding their kindness, their urge to communicate. Clumsily, they draw the signs of their feelings. Some people draw heart after heart, and—discreetly or indiscreetly—sing the praises of kindness. They have been wounded, and quite often they are glad of it; they have been pierced by the arrows of love. They do not want to be tough and unmoved. They accept themselves with all their weaknesses and tears.

On a wall in Montreal, just over a little red heart pierced by an arrow, one can barely make out another heart, pale, almost the same color as the wall. It is a sort of ghostly heart, a trace, almost utterly destroyed, of a love affair that no one may remember. Hearts accumulate. Multiple loves pile up side by side. Stories are proclaimed, but nobody is telling them. Perhaps they are true stories, perhaps only dreams. Often all that remains is four initials, referring to two unknown people.

An undefined tenderness is suggested by a heart, pierced or unpierced. Here, someone (nobody knows who, nobody knows when) thought he felt (more or less sincerely, more or less faithfully) love, reciprocated or not. He (or she) drew that love on a city wall, as others carve it into a school desk or on a tree trunk, as still others—caring less if it lasts, more accepting of the ephemeral nature of things—write it on a sandy beach, just before the sea comes in to wash it away.

We probably do not pay enough attention to these undefined feelings, these wandering declarations that are collected by the wall photographer. Graffiti suggest vague, anonymous desires, what one might call free-floating affection. Here—one might notice, in a rather unrevealing note—somebody loved. Along these streets, *there was once* a lover, perhaps two. And, this unspecified message is being sent out to no one in particular.

One may wonder at the many reasons that can drive men or women to write the sign of their tender feelings on a wall: is it like an oath calling the solid stone to witness? like the beginning of a story that they do not know whom to tell? like insurance against the indifference, the cruelty, of the city? We may also compare the hearts tattooed on walls and those tattooed on skin.

The heart is one of the most common images of popular iconography. Tracers of graffiti repeat themselves continually, for they have nothing against repetition. They have no desire to be avant-garde artists. They have no wish to invent, to find something new. Frequently, they quite naturally come upon the same figures, the same formulas. City walls are not often a place for inventiveness. But inventiveness is rare in most books and paintings, too. Besides, if inventiveness is fasci-

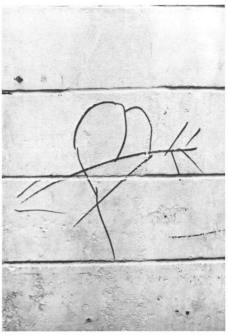

Geneva

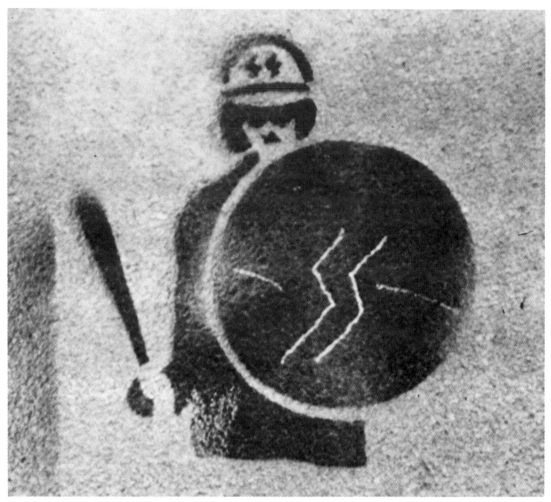

Zurich

To be or nato be

Zurich

Brussels

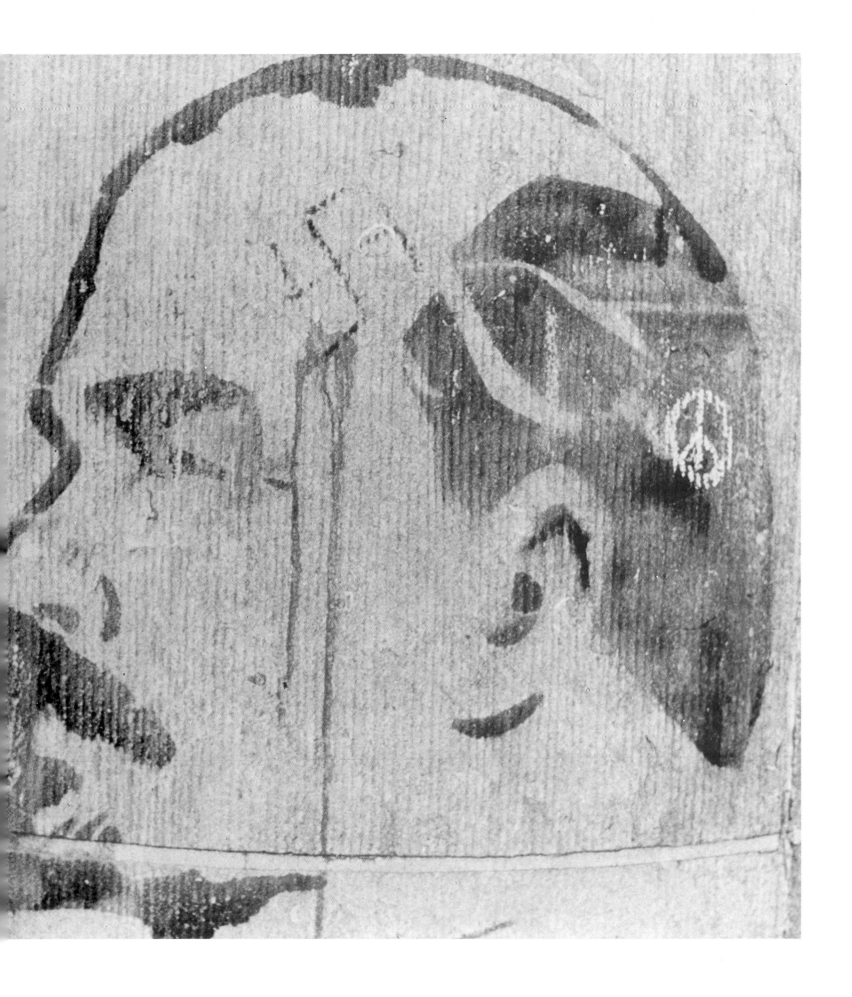

Geneva

nating, the repetition of forms can be moving; habit does not make things stale. To the lover who traces out a heart, the form has not become meaningless because others (and occasionally he himself) have already used it often. On the contrary. To him the heart is a powerful sign, a sign all the more effective because it refers to many other loves past and present. To him, the heart constitutes one of the letters of the alphabet of love, a letter that he can use felicitously again and again.

Sometimes, however, people who trace out a heart do show inventiveness; it comes into play to produce a *variation* based on a traditional form, modifying the form without seeking to do away with it. For example, one day—after twenty years of observation—Dogançay (with a pleasure beyond words) comes across a heart pierced by two arrows instead of one. Or, in Paris, someone replaces the slant of the arrow that usually pierces the heart by the slant of a hypodermic. So Cupid the Archer has become a drug user or a pusher; love has been linked to Baudelaire's "artificial paradises." Or perhaps the desire for heroin has become the only desire of the wall-writer—no longer the lover of woman but of hallucination.

Most hearts drawn on walls are merely outlined. However, in Tel Aviv, a red heart with a green background has been placed next to a green heart with a red background. Some viewers may think of a strange card game in which all the

Marburg

aces are hearts of various colors. Others will wonder if the red heart is masculine and the green heart feminine, or the other way around. Still others will see this play of colors as an expression of the wall-painter's sensitivity to art, stronger than in colorless graffiti.

Hands

Hands are certainly a bit less common than hearts. . . . On a Cairo wall, a red hand is partly hidden by a poster. It is a magical sign of protection. Or else, in its bloody red, it is a message of horror. Nobody knows. Nobody knows. Elsewhere, in France, traces of hands pile up next to a poster of the main left-wing trade union. In Jerusalem, three hands form a strange equilateral triangle.

Without realizing it, no doubt, anonymous artists of the twentieth century repeat the gestures of prehistoric times. In the Gargas Caves (in the Pyrenees) there are about one hundred fifty red and black hands. There are around fifty in El Castillo, a dozen or so in Tibiran and Pech-Merle. In other caves, handprints are isolated or occasionally form little groups. Some of them, found especially in the Rhône Valley, are positive tracings, obtained by slapping a paint-covered hand on the wall. Others are negatives, made by dabbing the color around a hand

Tel Aviv

Lisbon

stuck on the wall with its fingers spread out. As André Leroi-Gourhan points out in his *Préhistoire de l'Art Occidental*, in most cases the hands are too small to have belonged to men. Rather, they are the hands of women or children.

At Gargas, some of the hands have missing fingers or twisted joints. Scholars have tried to explain this as "ritual mutilation." Leroi-Gourhan has another explanation: as the back of the hand was applied to the wall, the individual curled one or two fingers down for unknown reasons.

Images on Untreated Surfaces

It is not only forms (particularly those of hands) which permit us to compare the graffiti on our walls to prehistoric cave paintings. The same technique of painting on an untreated surface used by the anonymous artists of the twentieth century was used by their very distant ancestors.

"Paleolithic rock paintings," says Meyer Schapiro, "were made on an unprepared surface, the rough wall of a cave; the irregularities of the earth and the rock can be seen through the image. The artist was working in a visual field with no established limits, and thought so little of the surface as a distinct background that he often painted his animal figure over a previously painted picture without erasing the first one, as if it were invisible to the viewer." This description could apply to the walls of our cities.

Such practices are the opposite of a tradition of treated, neutralized backgrounds which contrast with the figures. Some contemporary artists also reject this neutralization, this preparation of the background surface.

The Use of Chance

So it happens that an inscription, a figure, is composed by using what already existed. It takes into account what was on the wall; it combines it with its own features. It uses the uneven parts of the wall, its flaws, its previous inscriptions. This is one of the possible meanings—although not the only one—of the sentence written on a wall in May 1968: *Il faut systématiquement explorer le hasard* ("Chance must be systematically explored").

Here, too, unintentionally, without knowing it, with a sort of naiveté, our anonymous wall-writers are close to the work of a number of contemporary artists. It is well known that Francis Bacon, for example, tries to bring chance into the composition of his paintings when he squeezes the paint onto his hand and throws it on the partially painted canvas, or when he soaks rags in paint and rubs them over various parts of the work. Bacon cultivates the accident that can break up his usual way of seeing things and help him discover a new vision. He wants an accident and provokes it. He learns from it. "Starting from a spot, a mark," he says, he tries "to construct the appearance of the subject [he] would like to grasp."

In the same way, a graffitist may spontaneously compose his inscription by starting from a spot or a crack on the wall, or else by starting from someone else's half-covered writing, without erasing it.

West Berlin

Magic

If wall writings are games of chance, they also—as Dogançay and others help us to see—constitute magical practices, and they are more or less clearly perceived as such by their authors themselves. The act of drawing or writing on a wall one's desire for love or murder is often accompanied by the hope that this act will contribute to the fulfillment of that desire—the hope of making the desire work, in a sense. Spells and exorcisms rub shoulders on the walls, even if those who use them do not dare admit it to others. Unconsciously, concealed rituals can be sensed behind certain graffiti. The cry of hatred wants to *work*. On a poster, a politician's head is cut off, his eyes gouged out with a pencil or with fingernails. By drawing an arrow through a heart, the artist hopes to arouse the love of a woman who goes walking indifferently past the wall. Sometimes religious ideas seem to inspire wall-writers. In West Berlin, blue stars come out of a red crucified figure. In Brussels, a horned faun has a gigantic heart for a body: a form has been invented here, referring to a being in which its inventor may believe to some extent.

Minor Mythologies

Thus, minor mythologies, brief and unelaborated, are set down and erased. A free unicorn stands erect in the heart of the city. Snoopy looks at a heart. A strange face appears made of Anwar Sadat's eyes and forehead and Jimmy Carter's mouth: the result of two lacerated posters. Traced on with a stencil, the outline of a policeman with his shield, almost medieval, no doubt represents the face of the enemy. The melancholy head of an assassinated singer fades slowly from a wall. Current events, advertising, the movies, all suggest temporary heroes. And Walt Disney's animals are drawn by Indian children.

Paris

Madrid

Antwerp

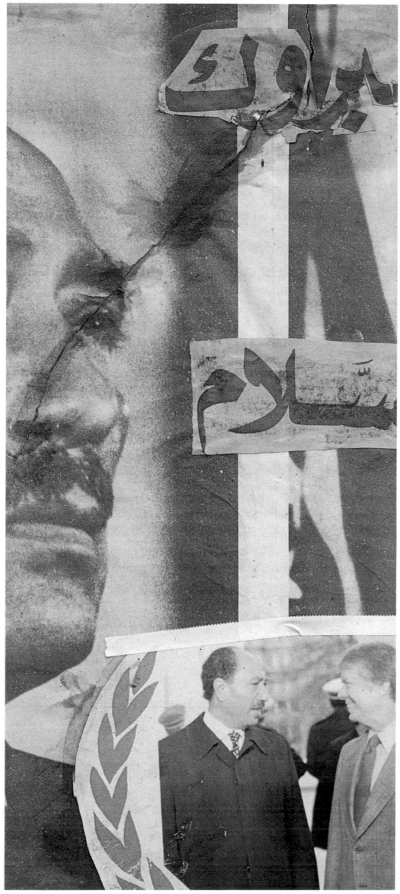

Cairo

Cairo

Toute personne a droit à la liberté de pensée, de conscience et de religion, la liberté d'expression et d'opinion

Brussels

On walls one can read how new mythologies are born. Characters are mixed in with signs: arrows, stars, crosses, and letters. To definite slogans are added elusive, sometimes incomprehensible narratives. Next to clear messages there spring up personal, puzzling stories, which are written down because they cannot be told aloud.

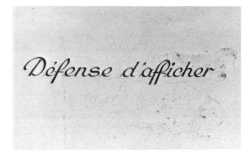

Geneva

The Hand-to-Hand Struggle with Matter, the Base

The graffiti-maker, like the caveman, like some contemporary artists, has a taste for close contact with the base, with matter. They all display the same urge to translate their ideas and whims with immediacy.

Jean Dubuffet wrote that it is a good thing to work "with your hands full." In 1945, just after the period in which he explored the city and captured, in his lithographs, the memory of ephemeral inscriptions, of scaling, spattered, slanting walls—the memory of the traces of poverty and war—he wrote: "The essential gesture of the painter is to smear. Not to spread out tinted water with a pen or a little bristle wick, but to plunge his hands into brimming buckets or basins and putty up the wall in front of him with earth and paste, to knead it in hand-to-hand combat, to print it with the most immediate possible marks of his thought and rhythms and the pulse throbbing in his arteries and running through his nervous system—barehanded, or using a few rudimentary tools that are good conductors, some chance blade or short stick or glass splinter...."

For Dubuffet, any painter could benefit by taking a lesson from the tracer of graffiti. He should prefer walls to canvas, the hand or the stick to the brush, the immediate response to slow meditation. He should learn to knead and dig, to seek out the hand-to-hand struggle with the surface to be covered, with the material he is using. He should distrust distance and delight in close contact.

Communication

Leaf through the thousands of wall photographs collected by Dogançay. Some will make you think, some will make you dream. For instance, you will think about the urge to communicate and about the fears that all too often accompany this desire.

When we look at the walls of the city, we encounter both the urge to communicate and the urge to break off communication, constantly intertwined. Walls separate individuals from each other; they are often the walls of a prison. They also serve as the basis for messages, for appeals. But the messages themselves are

Istanbul

Copenhagen

Rotterdam

often ambiguous, filled with hate. They often silence or disturb other messages: on walls, writers cut each other off. It even happens that certain appeals for love are unconsciously insults, ways of cutting the author off from others. Some sexual propositions are written on a wall so as not to be whispered to a live man or woman. And many are trying to shock far more than to seduce. When someone displays loneliness, that individual is not always seeking an encounter.

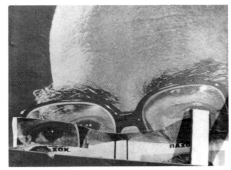

Athens

Sharing a Space

Or, study how individuals interrupt each other, in a sense, how often they fight with each other to try to be heard.

It would be pointless to seek a common philosophy in wall writings. Individual desires, minority demands, memories concerning now one person, now millions—all are scattered over walls. It may happen that twenty people have written their hopes and despair in a space of a few square yards. Whether they like it or not, they are sharing the space. In any case, they are taking it away from those who would like to keep it "clean."

Sometimes walls whisper. Sometimes tiny markings and graffiti seem to be in hiding. Sometimes they howl, enormous. Walls often express revolt, a desperate desire to be heard—to get a message across, but also quite simply to shout, to affirm one's existence when it feels threatened by institutions. At the Ecole des Langues Orientales, Paris, in May, 1968, an anonymous writer (who has remained so), states his/her desire not to be a mere number: *Je crie/j'écris/n° 595.378.822.334 bis de l'anonyme contrainte* ("I shout/I write out/nos. 595,378,822,334A of anonymous repression"). He/she demands the right to a name and does not give one.

At quite different moments, wall writings are paradoxical. May, 1968, on a wall in a lecture hall at the University of Paris-Nanterre: *J'aime pas écrire sur les murs* ("I don't like to write on walls"). At Paris-Censier: *J'ai quelque chose à dire, mais je ne sais pas quoi* ("I have something to say, but I don't know what it is"). Or, more mysteriously, someone writes to affirm the importance of silence or perhaps a love of nothingness: *Rien* ("Nothing"). Or, then again, someone opts for a violent tone, perhaps humorously, perhaps to criticize himself, or perhaps thinking he is giving the floor to his enemies: *Quels sont les porcs qui osent écrire sur les murs?* ("Who are the swine who dare to write on walls?").

The Clean and the Dirty

Thoughts about cleanliness and dirt come up often when one considers graffiti and posters. There are some who like walls clean and unmarked, who see

Milan

New York

Rio de Janeiro

in graffiti a lack of hygiene, a threat of chaos, a sign of revolt, a sort of exhibitionism that bothers them. Sometimes they describe wall writing as a leprous disease attacking their city.

Around 1931, Georges Bataille spoke of a "recourse to anything shocking, impossible to describe, or even abject . . ." He quoted Marx, for whom "in history as in nature, rotting is the laboratory of life." To accept and even to desire the way of dirtiness would be to find a path to freedom. On this question of the clean and the dirty, many other positions are possible.

Some see in the inscriptions on cracking walls a way of condemning the horror of the life they are forced to lead. Others see an attempt to cover up the unacceptable, to paint an ocean, flowers, a blue sky in places where dust, factory smoke, and crumbling bricks seem to make life and happiness impossible. Graffiti may be on the side of revolt, of camouflage, of condemnation, of insult, of defilement, of dreams of heaven. Walls may be what is hidden, what is made visible, what is accused or used. They become sets in a theater, or an immense protest, or a political publication.

In any case, the photographs of Dogançay, those of other photographers, as well as the work of certain artists, make us think through the concepts of the dirty and the clean, the new and the used, the varied nature of walls—all of which we often forget to consider.

They teach us to read the regularity of bricks, the rough surfaces more or less crumbling away, the posters more or less ripped apart, more or less spotted up. Often they help us to see the manifold effects of time. Painted letters peel off. The face of Mao Tse Tung fades away and leads us to see the splintery wood into which the poster has penetrated. Everywhere things are ripped up, fragmented, split apart. The future of walls and of what is written on them is, sooner or later, dust and oblivion.

Dates and Spelling

And then sometimes wall photographs can make you attentive to details. You wonder about the dates written on walls, about the relationship of graffiti to time.

In France, one date appears again and again on walls, sometimes half erased or crossed out: the date of a ban, the prohibition against "posting bills," the Law of July 29, 1881 (*Défense d'afficher, Loi du 29 juillet 1881*). Other dates are intended to commemorate the death of an activist or the birth of a love affair; still others call you to demonstrations: *Tous à la Bastille, le 15 mai 1970* ("Everyone to the

Paris

West Berlin

Caracas

Tunis

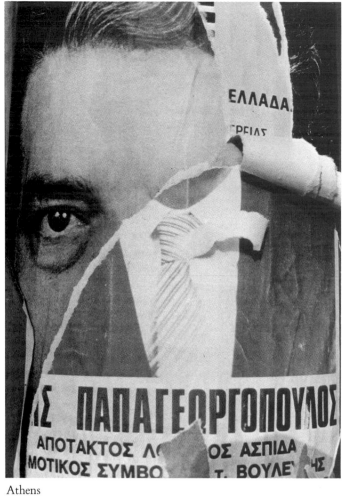

Athens

Brussels

New York

217

Paris

Bastille, May 15, 1970"). Sometimes walls function as a memorial, a monument to the dead and loved ones of the past. Or they hold the dreams of the future. Or, yet again, for a short moment, they enable people to prepare for political action, the organization of a march or a riot.

Sometimes the absence of a date creates strange situations. I know a wall on which this sentence has been left for more than five years: "Martine, meet us at the cafeteria."

You can also think about the spelling of certain graffiti. Some play with spelling: *Jém ékrir en fonétik* ("I like riting in fonetix") writes a student on a wall of the University of Paris-Censier. Others are in a hurry: they trace words on walls in constant fear that the police will arrive, or a group of opponents; they have no time to worry about spelling. Others have problems writing on a vertical surface; they learned to write on school desks, and another position of the hand disorients them and increases the chances for a mistake. In Brussels, a hand forgets an "i" and writes *Défense d'affcher* ("Post no blls"). Still others, conscious enemies of correct spelling, try to attack it, to hurt it. To them, spelling is on the side of the professors and the "haves," the mandarins: *L'orthographe est une mandarine* ("Spelling is a female mandarin"). Finally, there are others who do not know how to spell, but write anyway.

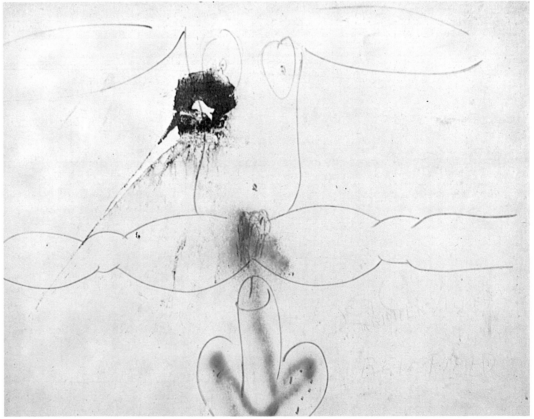

Rotterdam

Silhouettes

Or, you may be interested in silhouettes. On a Brussels wall appears the black silhouette of a little man in a bowler hat. You could think of a Magritte painting of a lover. You could think of Charlie Chaplin. You could see in this little faceless man the very image of all the anonymous people who humbly, modestly, obstinately write and draw on walls.

Elsewhere, in Marburg, the silhouettes of a man, a woman, a little girl, and a little boy are waving. Rejecting relief, shadows and reflections, the silhouette accepts the absence of depth. It immediately locates itself in a two-dimensional world. The silhouette depends on an emphasis on outline, with a provisional neglect of relief and lighting. It contrasts dark, monochromatic surfaces with a lighter background.

Such silhouettes on walls repeat—unknowingly—one of the mythical origins of painting. According to Pliny the Elder, the lovesick daughter of the potter Butades of Corinth looked at the shadow of her lover on the wall, and then, with a piece of coal, traced the line surrounding the shadow. She pinned down the ephemeral cast shadow. She stopped it in a silhouette. Here is the origin of painting, dreamed up from a story of love and walls. Leonardo da Vinci emphasized

Brussels

New York

Lisbon

Madrid

Montreal

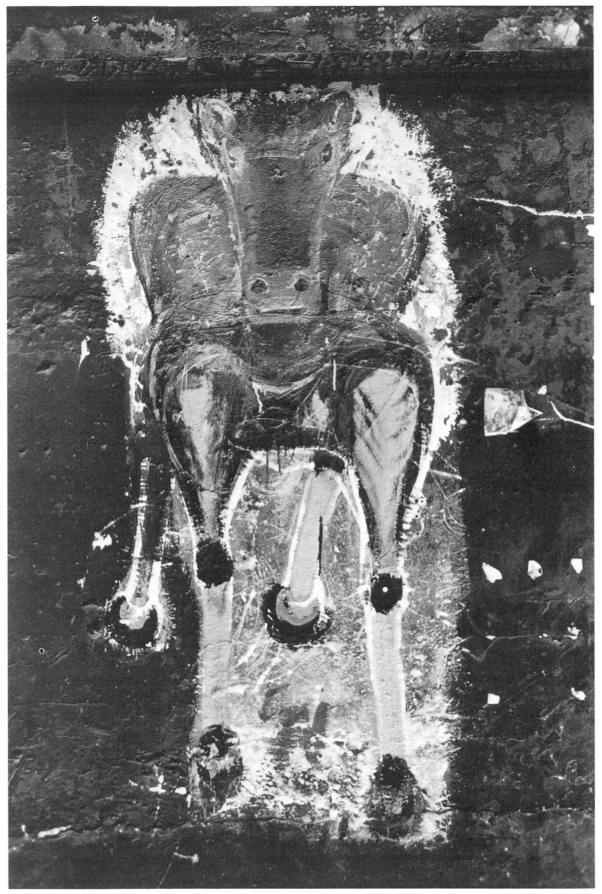

Paris

the source of light rather than the passions of the man or woman who painted: "The first picture was a single line drawn round the shadow of a man cast by the sun on the wall."

Humility and Glory

And then, at last, as you look at some of the twelve thousand photographs taken by Dogançay, you will think of the humility and glory of walls.

Of humility first. One of the forces of good in graffiti is their timidity. They are the almost imperceptible, often suppressed, voice of the insulted and the injured, of those whose voice has been stolen and who are sometimes driven out of their city. Graffiti are often written at night, very quickly, fearfully, by furtive passersby. They are exposed to the action of the wind and rain, rapidly erased, eliminated. But unceasingly, new, anonymous wall-writers pick up the torch, despite bans and bad weather.

The most modest graffiti are perhaps the most moving. They often transmit the messages of those who have no other form of action. In a sense, the wall itself becomes a place that shines out and moves those who look at it.

In May, 1968, in Entrance Hall A of the University of Paris-Nanterre, an anonymous individual admired—humorously or not, no one will ever know—the wall he or she was writing on: *Mur baignant infiniment dans sa propre gloire* ("Wall basking infinitely in its own glory"). There can be a kind of glory in a wall—a surface for inscriptions, an enormous place for drawing and writing—calling, in a sense, for the action of marking pencils and paint.

GILBERT LASCAULT

223

New York

Abidjan

Rabat

New York

London

Genoa

Stockholm

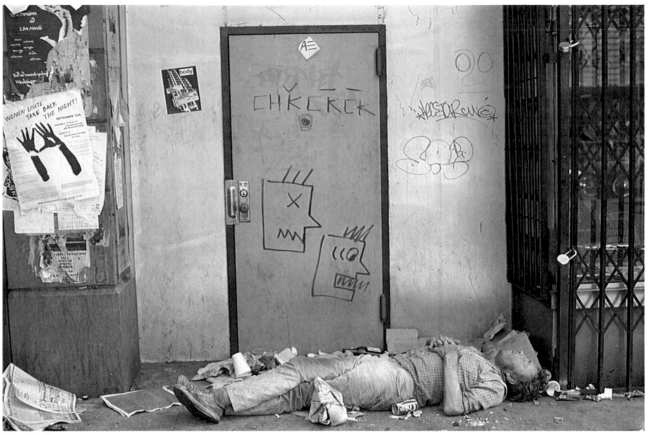

New York

New York

Paris

Zurich

West Berlin

Dakar

Vienna

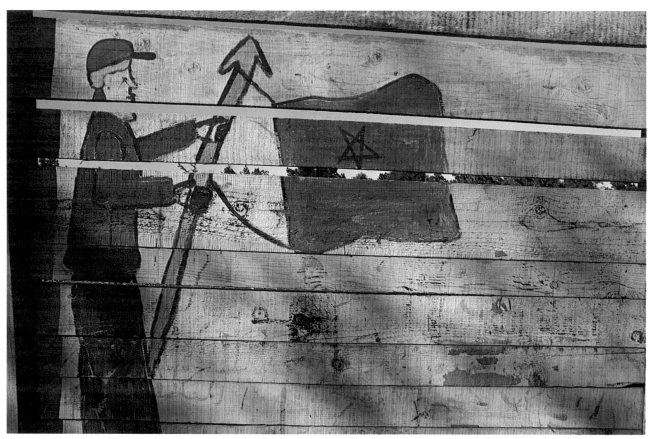

Rabat

Vienna

AFTERWORD

Now it is time for the reader to form his or her own opinion of Dogançay's work, wander back through this retrospective or simply close the book. Remember that in the contemporary art world, where "isms" and "ists" abound, and artists are grouped by critics and commentators into schools and movements, often before time has provided sufficient basis for insight and perspective, Dogançay has chosen to tread a lonely path through what he regards as "the new and violent movements of contemporary art."

Absorbed in extending the limits of his chosen subject, walls, he has unconsciously refused membership in what are regarded as the established schools of our time. Paradoxically, his individualism has not excluded him from the mainstream, where he is, after all, not alone. He shares in the major quest of most modern artists, always asking the question: where next?

Because Dogançay first came to this country in the early 1960s, it is not surprising that this artist with a compassionate eye and a need to read the pulse of society chose walls—speaking walls—as his subject. He arrived here in time to witness the human comedy of the 1960s when major upheavals were occurring at all levels in society. Walls were makeshift bulletin boards for the slogans, posters, and graffiti of the so-called "Now" generation, which laid bare its aspirations, ideals, and anguish.

The speaking wall is not, however, a period piece, restricted to any particular time or place. Dogançay observed during his journeys through Europe, Africa, and Asia that *all* walls have tales to tell. That the walls of the world speak a common language in differing patois is documented by the photographic archive he amassed during his travels, and later exhibited. These photographs provide germinal information about the artist's vision, his sensitivity, his humor. After all, the flicker of the camera's shutter may be said to parallel the blinking of the artist's own eye. Dogançay's photographs of walls are the seeds for his paintings and sculpture. If these photographs are the vernacular of his work, his paintings and sculpture are undoubtedly its lingua franca.

Never preoccupied simply with amusing or sentimental slogans and graffiti, or sidetracked by superficially arresting textures and shapes, Dogançay's work has kept its momentum. The speaking walls that at first provided inspiration, as well as a focal point of reference, have now become membrane-like divisions between inner and outer space. Ribbon-like shapes, which derive their power from some unseen inner space, reach out into *our* space, casting shadows in strange hues of purple and blue. Just how far this idée fixe would take him has always been Dogan-çay's major consideration: at this point the answer appears to be infinity.

CLIVE GIBOIRE

CHRONOLOGY

1929
Born in Istanbul

1950
Enrolled at the Faculté de Droit de l'Université de Paris

1953
Received doctorate in economics

1955
Returned to Turkey to work for the government

1958
Appointed director of Turkish pavilion at the Brussels World Fair

1959
Became director of the Department of Tourism
Visited the U.S.A. for the first time

1962
Appointed director of Turkish Information and Tourism Office in New York City

1964
Exhibited at Ward Eggleston Galleries, New York—first one-man show
Resigned from government service to devote himself fully to art
Awarded Certificate of Appreciation by the City of New York

1965
Honored by the first inclusion of his work in a public collection
(The Solomon R. Guggenheim Museum)

1969
Received Tamarind Lithography Workshop Fellowship, Los Angeles

1974
Selected to contribute a UNICEF card design

1976-77
Lived in Switzerland and traveled for Walls of the World photographic project

1978
Returned to New York City
Married Angela Hausmann

1979

Became an American citizen

1982

Exhibited at Centre Georges Pompidou, Paris, as special guest of French government

1983

Named Painter of the Year in Turkey by *Ev & Ofis*

Invited to supply tapestry designs to the Atelier Raymond Picaud, Aubusson

Introduced Alucobond Shadow Sculpture

1984

Won Enka Arts and Science Award, Istanbul

Continued Walls of the World photographic project in North and West Africa

1986

Represented Turkey in the 1st International Asian-European Art Biennial, Ankara

EXHIBITIONS

ONE-MAN EXHIBITIONS

1956   Ankara: Sanatsevenler Kulübü

1957   Ankara: Sanatsevenler Kulübü

1958   Ankara: Sanatsevenler Kulübü

1959   Ankara: Sanatsevenler Kulübü

1964   New York: Ward Eggleston Galleries
New York: Berlitz Gallery
New York: Overseas Club

1965   New York: Ward Eggleston Galleries
Phoenix: Galaxy Gallery

1966   New York: American Greetings Gallery

1967   New York: Spectrum Gallery

1968   Cambridge: Radcliffe Graduate Center

1969   New York: Spectrum Gallery

1970   New York: Carus Gallery
Washington, D.C.: Lunn Gallery

1971   New York: J. Walter Thompson Company

1973   New York: Gimpel & Weitzenhoffer Gallery
Rockford: Sneed & Hillman Gallery

1976   Istanbul: Galeri Baraz

1977   Istanbul: Galeri Baraz
Stockholm: Galleri Engström
Zurich: Kunstsalon Wolfsberg

1978   New York: The Turkish Center
New York: Gimpel & Weitzenhoffer Gallery
Gotenborg: Galleri Olab

1981   Sarasota: Foster Harmon Galleries
Zurich: Kunstsalon Wolfsberg

1982   Paris: Centre Georges Pompidou
Brussels: Palais des Beaux-Arts
Hasselt: Provinciaal Museum Hasselt
Antwerp: I.C.C.
Chambéry: C.A.U.E.
Nice: Maison des Jeunes & de la Culture Magnan
Oyonnax: Secrétariat à l'action culturelle
Cologne: Baukunst-Galerie

1983   Lons-le-Saunier: M.J.C.
Pont-à-Mousson: Centre Culturel de l'Ancienne Abbaye des Prémontrés
Le Vaudreuil: Collectif d'Animation de la Ville
Metz: Conseil d'Architecture, d'Urbanisme et de l'Environnement
Moulins: Direction Départementale de l'Equipement de l'Allier
Montreal: Musée d'Art Contemporain
Istanbul: Galeri Baraz
Bordeaux: Café Librarie Vent Debout

1984	Reims: Centre Saint-Exupéry
	Rennes: MJC-Auberge de la Jeunesse/Maison pour Tous
	Vienne: MJC-Auberge de la Jeunesse/Maison pour Tous
	Bagnères-de-Bigorre: Bibliothèque Municipale
	Caen: MJC La Guérinière
	Chamalières: A.E.D.A.P.
	Dusseldorf: Galerie Swidbert
	Alfortville: Maison des Jeunes et de la Culture
	Ankara: Vakko Sanat Galerisi
	Istanbul: Vakko Sanat Galerisi
	Izmir: Vakko Sanat Galerisi
1985	Bordeaux: Centre d'Art et de Communication
	Sarasota: Foster Harmon Galleries
	Rabat: Galerie l'Atelier
	Vienna: Österreichische Postsparkasse

GROUP EXHIBITIONS

1953 Paris: Fondation des Etats-Unis. *Exposition des Peintres Résidants de la Fondation des Etats-Unis*

1959 Ankara: Turkish-American Association. *Painters of Ankara*

1961 Ankara: Turkish-American Association. *Exhibition of Modern Paintings organized by Art Critics*
Ankara: University of Ankara. *The Twenty-Second State Exhibition of Painting and Sculpture*

1963 New York: Washington Square Galleries. *World Show*
New York: The National Arts Club. *The 64th Anniversary Exhibition*

1964 New York: The National Arts Club. *The 65th Anniversary Exhibition*

1965 Monaco: Palais des Congrès. *Exposition Intercontinentale*
New York: Gallery of Modern Art. *About New York: 1915–1965*
New York: The Solomon R. Guggenheim Museum. *Some Recent Gifts*

1970 New York: Union Carbide Galleries. *Contemporary Turkish Artists*

1971 Binghamton: University Art Gallery, State University of New York at Binghamton
Contemporary Turkish Painting, an exhibition which traveled to:
Chicago: University of Chicago;
Minneapolis: Minneapolis College of Art and Design;
New York: Finch College Museum of Art, Contemporary Wing. *Artists at Work*

1971-72 New York: Pace Gallery. *Printmakers at Pace*

1975 New York: The Solomon R. Guggenheim Museum. *Recent Acquisitions*

1977 Istanbul: Galeri Baraz. *Sabri Berkel, Burhan Dogançay, B. Rahmi Eyuboglu, Fikret Mualla*
New York: The Solomon R. Guggenheim Museum. *From the American Collection*
New York: Union Carbide Building. *Artists 77*

1980 Rockford: Sneed Gallery. *Small Works by Big Artists*
Chicago: Mary Bell Galleries. *New Works by Gallery Artists*

1982 Cologne: Baukunst-Galerie

1982-83 National traveling exhibition: *The Heritage of Islam*
Houston: The Houston Museum of Natural Science
San Francisco: The California Academy of Sciences
Washington, D.C.: The National Museum of Natural History, Smithsonian Institution

1983 Istanbul: Alarko Art Gallery. *Fifty Rare Turkish Paintings of This Century*
Zurich: Kunstsalon Wolfsberg

1984 Rockford: Sneed Gallery. *Who's New and What's New*
Sarasota: Foster Harmon Galleries. *Major American Artists*

1985 La Tronche/Grenoble: Maison des Artistes-Fondation Herbert d'Uckermann.
Itinéraire d'une Galerie
Montreux: Palais des Congrès. *Les chefs-d'oeuvre d'Aubusson*

PUBLIC AND CORPORATE COLLECTIONS

Austria	Vienna: Österreichische Postsparkasse Vienna: Museum Moderner Kunst Wattens: Swarovski
Belgium	Antwerp: Musées Royaux des Beaux-Arts Ghent: Museum van Hedendaagse Kunst Latem Saint Martin: Musée d'Art Contemporain Liège: Musée d'Art Moderne Ostend: Musée d'Ostend
Brazil	Rio de Janeiro: Museu de Arte Moderna do Rio de Janeiro
Canada	Toronto: University of Toronto Victoria: Museum of Greater Victoria
France	Paris: Musée d'Art Moderne de la Ville de Paris Strasbourg: Musée d'Art Moderne
Israel	Dimona: Musée de la Ville de Dimona Jerusalem: Bezalel National Art Museum
Switzerland	Zurich: Kronenhalle Zurich: Swiss Aluminium Ltd.
Turkey	Istanbul: Güzel Sanatlar Akademisi Istanbul: Resim ve Heykel Müzesi Istanbul: Enka Holding Inc.
United States	Athens: Georgia Museum of Art, The University of Georgia Athens: The Ohio University College of Fine Arts Boston: American Airlines Chicago: CNA Financial Corp. Chicago: First National Bank of Chicago Chicago: The Sears Building Fort Worth: Amon Carter Museum of Western Art Fredonia: State University College, Michael C. Rockefeller Arts Center La Jolla: La Jolla Museum of Art Lincoln: De Cordova and Dana Museum and Park Los Angeles: The Benjamin and Dorothy Smith Foundation Los Angeles: Grunwald Center for the Graphic Arts, UCLA Los Angeles: Los Angeles County Museum of Art Los Angeles: University of California at Los Angeles Art Galleries Lynchburg: Randolph-Macon Woman's College Art Gallery Newark: The Newark Museum Newark: Prudential Insurance Company New York: Allen & Co. New York: The Brooklyn Museum New York: The Museum of Modern Art New York: The Museum of the City of New York New York: The Solomon R. Guggenheim Museum

New York: J. Walter Thompson Company
New York: The Chase Manhattan Bank, N.A.
New York: Citibank, N.A.
New York: MHT Co.
New York: RCA Corp.
Notre Dame: The Snite Museum of Art, The University of Notre Dame
Rockford: Clark Arts Center, Rockford College
Rockford: Burpee Art Museum
Saint Louis: Webster College
Sarasota: John & Mable Ringling Museum of Art
Washington, D.C.: Library of Congress

Yugoslavia   Skopje: Musée d'Art Contemporain

BIBLIOGRAPHY

"Açılış Tablosus Yapıldı." *Hürriyet*, Istanbul, October 6, 1983

Allyn, Rex. "A Chance for Leisurely Study of Art Works." *Sarasota Herald Tribune*, Sarasota, July 15, 1984

Allyn, Rex. "Harmon Features Internationally Known Artists." *The Longboat Observer*, Sarasota, February 21, 1985

"Altin Palet Büyük Onur Ödülü." *Sanat Çevresi*, Istanbul, no. 60, October 1983

Asselin, Hedwige, "Les Murs du Monde." *Le Devoir*, Montreal, July 30, 1983

Bartlett, Maxine. "Devoted Turkish Diplomat Shows Artistic Talents." *The Arizona Republic*, Phoenix, January 23, 1965

Berkand, Necdet. "Yeni Dünya'da Bir Sanat Elçimiz." *Tercüman*, Istanbul, June 10, 1969

Bilgin, Çetin. "Duvarların Dili." *Ankara Siyasi Halk Gazetesi*, Istanbul, September 7, 1976

Bowles, Jerry and Russell, Tony. "Walls 70, Burhan Dogançay." *This Book is a Movie*. New York: Dell, 1971

"Burhan Dogançay." *The New York Herald Tribune*, New York, April 11, 1964

"Burhan Dogançay." *The New York Herald Tribune*, New York, April 3, 1965

"Burhan Dogançay." *Politika*, Istanbul, August 18, 1976

"Burhan Dogançay." *Die Tat*, Zurich, February 2, 1977

"Burhan Dogançay: Wände der Welt." *Litfass*, Berlin, no. 16, April 1980

"Burhan Dogançay." Kunstsalon Wolfsberg, Zurich, 1981

"Burhan Dogançay: Duvarlar Ve Resimler." *Boyut*, Ankara, November 1982

"Burhan Dogançay." *Nieuwe Gazet*, Antwerp, December 8, 1982

"Burhan Dogancay." *Ev & Ofis*, Istanbul, no. 87, November 1983

"Burhan Dogançay Monografisi." *Sanat Çevresi*, Istanbul, no. 61, November 1983

"Burpee Receives Dogançay Painting." *Register Star*, Rockford, January 6, 1974

C.G. "Burhan Dogançay." *Arts Magazine*, New York, December/January, 1968

Corbino, Marcia. "On the Wall Paintings." *Sarasota Herald Tribune*, Sarasota, February 9, 1981

Darcy, C. "Iere Exposition Intercontinentale à Monaco." *La Revue Moderne*, Paris, August 1, 1965

Dean, Kevin. "A Conversation with Burhan Dogançay." *The Longboat Observer*, Sarasota, February 5, 1981

Dean, Kevin. "Art/Foster Harmon Gallery." *The Longboat Observer*, Sarasota, February 21, 1985

Dogançay, Burhan. "Paradoxe." *Les Murs Murmurent, Ils Crient, Ils Chantent . . .*, Centre Georges Pompidou/CCI, Paris, 1982

Dormen, Haldun. "Uluslararası Bir Türk Ressamı." *Milliyet*, Istanbul, May 8, 1977

Dunn, Helen. "Burhan Dogançay: Artist, Photographer." *People, Places and Parties*, New York, Summer, 1982

Elibal, Gültekin. "Burhan Dogançay'ın Bir Sergisi Daha." *Sanat Çevresi*, Istanbul, no. 61, November 1983

Ervefel. "Burhan Dogançay." *La Semaine d'Anvers*, Antwerp, December 17, 1982

Gillemon, Danièle. "La Photographie Existe." *Le Soir*, Brussels, April 2, 1982

Grasskamp, Walter. *Kunstforum International*. Cologne, vol. 50, April 1982

Halman, Talat. "Burhan Dogançay New Yorkta Sergi Açtı." *Milliyet*, Istanbul, November 25, 1967

Halman, Talat. "Burhan Dogançay." *Ankara Sanat Dergisi*, Ankara, March 1977

Halman, Talat. "Amerika'da Modern Türk Sanatı." *Türk Evi*, New York, November 1977

"Harmon Combines Burhan Dogançay, Robert Watson and Group Exhibit." *Sarasota Herald Tribune*, Sarasota, February 17, 1985

H. N. "Burhan Dogançay." *Die Tat*, Zurich, February 28, 1977

Jacobs, Jay. "Personality: Back to the Walls." *The Art Gallery Magazine*, Ivoryton, vol. XIV, no. 1, October 1970

J.D.H. "Dogançay's Watercolors at Galaxy." *The Arizona Republic*, Phoenix, January 31, 1965

J.L. "Murmures des Murs." *La Presse*, Montreal, July 30, 1983

Köksal, Ahmet. "Dogançay'in Resimleri." *Milliyet, Sanat Dergisi*, Istanbul, September 17, 1976

Köprülü, Tuna. "Sanatımızı Dogançay ile Dünyaya Duyuruyoruz." *Hürriyet*, Istanbul, June 23, 1982

"Kunst in Zürich." *Neue Zürcher Zeitung*, Zurich, October 9, 1981

Lascault, Gilbert. "Ébauche d'un Dictionnaire des Murs et Graffiti." *Les Murs Murmurents, Ils Crient, Ils Chantent...*, Centre Georges Pompidou/CCI, Paris, 1982

"Les Murs Murmurent."*Le Républicain Lorrain*, Pont-à-Mousson, February 3, 1983

"Les Murs Murmurent: Les Photos Insolites." *L'Est Républicain*, Pont-à-Mousson, February 2, 1983

"Les Murs Murmurent, Ils Crient, Ils Chantent." *La Vie Nouvelle*, Chambéry, November 12, 1982

Levick, L.E. "Burhan Dogançay." *New York Journal American*, New York, April 11, 1964

Lieber, Joel. "Travel of Turkish Tourist Head Forms Inspiration for Painting." *Travel Weekly*, New York, June 9, 1964

Madra, Beral. "Burhan Dogançay'in Resimleri Üzerine." *Sanat Çevresi*, Istanbul, no. 61, November 1983

M.B. "Burhan Dogançay: Walls V." *Arts Magazine*, New York, March 1969

Messer, Thomas M. "Matériaux Bruts." *Les Murs Murmurents, Ils Crient, Ils Chantent...*, Centre Georges Pompidou/CCI, Paris, 1982

Meyer, Walter. "Handwriting on a Wall Tells Artist Great Deal." *Sunday News*, New York, September 18, 1966

Miller, Marlan. "Diplomat Offers Dashing Shows." *The Phoenix Gazette*, Phoenix, February 1, 1965

M. M. C. "New York in the Eyes of the World." *The Villager*, New York, October 1, 1964

Mullender, Jacques. "Les Murs, Instruments et Miroirs du Hasard." *Les Murs Murmurent, Ils Crient, Ils Chantent...*, Centre Georges Pompidou/CCI, Paris, 1982

Mûuls, Violaine. "On Baîllonne Même les Murs." *L'Evénement*, Brussels, no. 102, March 25, 1982

Noel, Serge. "L'Image a des Ratés." *Pour Bruxelles*, Brussels, March 25, 1982

"One-Man Exhibits to Open." *Sarasota Herald Tribune*, Sarasota, February 1, 1981

"Paintings by Dogançay in Pan Am Spotlight," *Brooklyn Bay News*, New York, September 17, 1966

Pak, Orhan. "Amerika'da Bir Türk Ressamı: Burhan Dogançay." *Sanat Çevresi*, Istanbul, July 1982

"Peinture: Burhan Dogançay." *Le Matin du Sahara*, Rabat, March 5, 1985

"Photographie: Du Souvenir à l'Image."*Pourquoi Pas?*, Brussels, April 1, 1982

P. WD. "Januaris/Dogançay/Zeller." *Neue Zürcher Zeitung*, Zurich, February 8, 1977

Reisner, Robert. *Graffiti*. New York: Cowles, 1971

Rigaud, Jacques. "Murs Murmurent." *Les Murs Murmurent, Ils Crient, Ils Chantent...*, Centre Georges Pompidou/CCI, Paris, 1982

Schutz, Louise B. "Burhan Dogançay: The Man and his Art." Thesis, Randolph-Macon Woman's College, Lynchburg, June 1971

Shemanski, Frances. "Diplomatic Mission." *Pictorial Living–New York Journal American*, New York, January 3, 1965

Simavi, Aliye. "Burhan Dogançay." *Vizon Gazete*, Istanbul, October 1980

Tansug, Sezer. "Burhan Dogançay'la Söylesiden Izlenimler." *Sanat Çevresi*, Istanbul, September 1979

Tansug, Sezer. "Büyük Bir Resim Ustası: Burhan Dogançay." *Sanat Çevresi*, Istanbul, no. 61, November 1983

Tansug, Sezer. "Büyük Bir Usta: Burhan Dogançay." *Ev & Ofis*. Istanbul, no. 87, November 1983

"Turkish Delight." *Interior Design*, New York, February 1965

"Turkish Diplomat in New York is Artist of Note." *The Observer*, Nashville, May 28, 1964

"The Two Worlds of Burhan Dogançay." *The Travel Agent*, New York, July 25, 1964

Uluç, Dogan. "Dogançay ile Bir Söyleşi." *Dünya*, Istanbul, July 17, 1979

Uluç, Dogan. "Açık Oturum." *Hürriyet*, Istanbul, November 3, 1982

Van Der Brempt, S. "La Photographie: Grand 'Art Nouveau.'" *La Semaine d'Anvers*, Antwerp, no. 336, April 16, 1982

"Wall Preserver." *Sunday News*, New York, October 9, 1966

"Walls 70: A Powerful Pastiche," *Interiors Magazine*, New York, December 1970

"Wandmalereien." *Zürichsee Zeitung*, Zurich, February 14, 1977

Wanfors, Lars. "American Graffiti." *American Trend Magazine*, Stockholm, no. 3, 1983

Welch, Anita. "Artist Captures Tempo of Manhattan." *The Arizonian*, Phoenix, January 28, 1965

"Yirmi Küsur Yildan Beri Duvarlari Ciziyorum." *Cumhüriyet*, Istanbul, November 2, 1984

Interviews

Adams, Cindy. WABC Television, New York, September 15, 1966

O'Brian, Jack. WOR Radio, New York, October 12, 1966

CONTRIBUTORS

David Ball is a translator and poet who teaches at Smith College, Northampton.

Stephen DiLauro is a poet, author, and editor.

Angela Doançay holds an M.A. from The City University of New York, and is a graduate of the University of Geneva's School for Translating and Interpreting, Geneva.

Clive Giboire is a writer, author, lecturer, and producer of art books.

Gilbert Lascault is a noted French critic and writer.

Thomas M. Messer is director of the Solomon R. Guggenheim Foundation, New York.

Roy Moyer is Chief Design Officer for UNICEF and former director of the American Federation of Arts.

Jacques Rigaud is president of the Musée d'Orsay, Paris.

Marcel van Jole is president of the Museum of Contemporary Art, Antwerp, and a member of the International Association of Art Critics.